For the Joy of Obeying

Jason David Eubanks, MD

Copyright © 2019 Dawn Treader, LLC.

All rights reserved.

ISBN: 978-1-7325322-1-2

All Scripture references taken from the NIV translation
(Unless otherwise noted)

Dedication

For Elise and Adele—
May you find the joy of obeying our *Abba*.

For Josephine "Joy" Jefferies—
Your life of faithfulness brought a smile of joy to our
Father and all those blessed to know you.

Contents

Foreword   i

Author's Note   v

	Introduction: The Germination of Joy	1
1	The Promise of Blessing	8
2	Fear: Standing in Awe	17
3	Pain: The Great Teacher	25
4	Shame: The Voice of the Godly Conscience	34
5	Duty: Moral Obligation	42
6	The Great "Because…"	51
7	The Wind and the Waves	59
8	Agape: The Beloved's Love	68
9	Joy: The Top of Heaven's Stairway	77

Foreword

Some words seldom show up in the same sentence and more rarely stand side by side. *Joy* and *obedience* are such a pair. Why would anyone tether unbridled happiness with the need to submit and comply? It seems akin to trying to get a glass of bubbling champagne back into the uncorked bottle.

During the time Jason was writing *For the Joy of Obeying*, I had opportunity to rethink this relationship between *joy* and *obedience*. Two of us in his family were training puppies. Joy overflowed in prancing paws, wagging tails, floppy ears and face-licking kisses. Obedience, by contrast, was a war of wills. Pockets full of treats did not always deter simple distractions like a shoe to chew or a scurrying squirrel. Nothing in these early months of training would lead me to pair *joy* and *obedience* in the title of a book!

Jason, however, is bit of a dog whisperer. Winning a pet's love and respect is an art form for him. After three labs and now his vizsla, Zeke, it still awes me to watch him call his dog. At the sound of his name, Zeke sprints to him (usually over 30 mph) and comes to a sharp halt at his feet. He then stares Jason full in the face before lathering him with affection. What better image could you have of the *joy of obeying*?

While Jason makes joyful obedience look easy, what forces are at work here? Is it just a matter of training, time, and lots of treats? Or, is there a deeper, more primal motivator that builds these bonds of respect? Some trainers think fear—use of shock and e-collars—is essential to establish who is the master. Others believe praise and rewards are the keys to nurture obedience. They offer real chicken if dog treats cease to work.

This contrast in leadership styles is clear. But, when it comes to God winning our hearts so that we follow Him, how does He go about teaching us to obey? Does He favor fear or rewards? Might this differ for each of us? What is His ultimate goal?

The body of the book explores these questions as Jason offers insightful examples that range from a bitter Job, a rebellious Saul, a repentant David, and a reluctant Naaman, to others, who like Jesus' mother Mary, are responsive from the start. I especially appreciate that Jason shows how God's methods of training vary with character and specific context. Understanding that God longs to write His name of love on each heart, Jason's examples reveal God works in ways to match individual temperaments and the times.

The focus on HOW God trains us is, however, only part of Jason's concern. The underlying question propelling the book tracts the pulse of a more haunting question: WHY obey at all? What is the motivation? Even more basic, "WHO" and "WHAT" will you choose to obey? In a post-modern world that daily offers examples of apparent happiness and success based on self-constructed, non-biblical patterns of living, Jason asks: Is there any reason to obey God's laws?

While the question is age-old, the roots of its inquiry stem from a personal cry. That is what makes the book so vital. Jason tackles the same heartache the psalmist David rails against in Psalm 73: "Have I kept my heart pure in vain," because the wicked prosper and the obedient "suffer every morning new punishments"(Ps 73:13-14)? As the "prosperity of the wicked" so obviously abounds today, and consequences of sin are often so delayed they seem unattached, why obey?

Even more troubling is the problem presented by the plight of the older son in the parable of the prodigal. Simply put: If forgiveness is offered to all regardless of the path they have taken, why not enjoy wealth, women and wine as the younger son does? If a ring, a robe, a feast and the Father's embrace await us regardless of how we choose to live, why work to obey (what some would consider) God's "outdated" laws?

In *For the Joy of Obeying,* I hear Jason writing the unwritten journey of the prodigal's older brother—a journey that begins when his equation of obedience and blessing is blown apart by the Father's forgiving embrace of his younger brother. While the prodigal's temptations are largely physical and his failure as palpable as a pigpen, the journey of the older son is interior. He must confront the incalculable equation of God's love as it balances justice and mercy in a timeline that tests human patience and denies easy answers.

Like many believers, Jason bought the roundtrip ticket for this journey and found pure joy in his homecoming. You will hear in the following pages the warmth and wisdom in the Father's embrace of an older son who returns and sees God for who He really is: Everything. "All that I have ever had is yours."

If this Master has won your heart with love, you will run as joyfully to Him as Zeke sprints to Jason. As you stare in God's face and find your rest in Him, you will understand and rejoice in *"the joy of obeying."*

Gail K. Eubanks, PhD.

Editor, *For the Joy of Obeying*

Author's Note

This is a book about finding joy in obedience to God. Only a brokenness reclaimed by Love can tell that story.

I am one of the broken, bound together and given new life. I am failure, forgiven and redeemed by Love. I am a once willful child whose tears have been embraced by a Father who calls me "Beloved."

I am Peter, a well-intentioned, yet fumbling fool in the pre-dawn darkness. Now forgiven, I "cannot help speaking about what [I] have seen and heard"(Acts 4:20). I am Paul, once full of a misguided zeal. Now transformed, I am "crucified with Christ and I no longer live, but Christ lives in me"(Gal 2:20).

And Christ's love—the love that transformed me and changed the world—compels me to speak about the One I adore (2 Cor 5:14). For the *joy of obeying* I give you this story of love.

—J. D. Eubanks, MD

Joy, beautiful sparkle of God....
Joy is the name of the strong spring
In eternal nature.
Joy, joy drives the wheels
In the great clock of worlds.
She lures flowers from the buds,
Suns out of the firmament,
She rolls spheres in the spaces
That the seer's telescope does not know.

—Friedrich Schiller
"Ode to Joy," 1785

Introduction
The Germination of Joy

*...where morning dawns and evening fades
you [Lord] call forth songs of joy.*
—*Psalm 65:8*

In the backseat of my sister's Honda, I sandwiched myself between my two beautiful nieces. As our playful banter and conversation about our Saturday turned, we stumbled upon the unlikely topic of obedience. Because I love the honesty and clarity of children in the face of a question—no matter how big or small—I couldn't resist asking the girls: "What does it mean to *obey*?" Addie, eight years old, responded, "To do what you are told." "But why do we *obey*?" I followed. She responded: "To be a nice person. Because if I do it, I might get something good." Elise, her older sister, chimed in: "Because it is the right thing to do. To be a good person."

Much to the delight of their parents, neither of the girls answered my inquiry with a response rooted in fear or punishment. And yet, when I later posed similar questions to a group of work colleagues, the answers were predictably more varied. Obedience to them was more closely related to following a set of rules. The reasons for obeying ranged from fear of consequences to reward, shame, and even respect.

This variation in the understanding and appreciation of obedience reveals its layered complexity in our lives. What it means to *obey* may change as we mature. In a similar way, our conception of obedience, like most things, is also influenced by the forces that mold our lives: parents, religion, legislation, life experiences, social norms, etc.

But for most of us, our understanding of obedience rarely involves the idea of *joy*—a deep-seated feeling of great pleasure and inner rejoicing. If it does elicit joy, however, it is likely only in select categories or moments of our lives. For instance, we might have little trouble obeying the injunctions of a probate court when we know an inherited fortune awaits us. But when it comes to the everyday, who among us does not bristle when we are told we must *obey* unconditionally in all things at all times?[1]

Indeed, if we are honest, most of us downright hate the idea of obeying. We know obedience requires submission. It implies a subjugation of self-interest to a higher power or authority. And whether we act like stomping two-year-olds in diapers, rebellious teenagers, or more seasoned adults attempting to kneel our lives before God, this necessity to "bow down" often grates the inner person.

Not surprisingly, therefore, as the contemporary culture increasingly embraces an unrestrained "ME," obedience is viewed negatively. It is incorrectly seen as an impediment to "self." It is pejoratively portrayed as narrow-minded, restrictive, and unnecessary. It is unfairly maligned as unloving.

Perhaps as a trickle-down result of this cultural thinking, the Church has, in places, become less forthright in its emphasis on obedience in our lives. Consequently, many Christians approach the topic of obeying with a blasé nonchalance. Amidst this confused indifference, godly obedience then unwittingly finds

---

[1] Soren Kierkegaard, *The Lily of the Field and the Bird of the Air* (Princeton: Princeton University Press, 2016), 45.

itself hijacked by the extremes. At one end lies the "chains" of legalism; at the other, the folly of spiritual lawlessness. As C.S. Lewis reminds us: "That is the Devil getting at us. He always sends errors into the world in pairs—pairs of opposites." It is Satan's genius to cause us to rely on "our extra dislike of one error to draw [us] gradually into the opposite one."[2] He delights in our confusion!

This lack of spiritual clarity is only encouraged by the Church's growing propensity for a "consumerist mentality," where the gospel message is carefully packaged to appeal to the most, while offending the least.[3] What results is a focus almost entirely on love and grace, sometimes to the near exclusion of obedience and other hard, scriptural truths. A story of effusive love and undeserved grace meets less resistance.

Yet, while God's unrelenting love and amazing grace are the undeniable core of His redemptive story for us (and must be celebrated and preached!), they do *not* erase or replace the Lord's heart for obedience in our lives. Indeed, the same God who tells us He loves us, tells us we must *obey*! We are instructed: "Love the Lord your God and keep His requirements, His decrees, His laws and His commands *always*"(Deut 11:1).

As Christians we cannot live with blatant disregard or casual indifference to God's commands. When we do, we demonstrate an insincere love for God and an unfamiliarity with His Word. We forget: The God whose love sent us Jesus to die for our sins is the very same God whose demand for obedience sends a decimating, sulfurous rain on Sodom, opens up the

---

[2] C.S. Lewis, *Mere Christianity* (New York: HarperCollins, 1980), 186.

[3] Francis Chan, *Letters to the Church* (Colorado Springs: David C Cook, 2018), 53.

earth to swallow the insolent, and says to us all, "'Consider...you who forget God, or I will tear you to pieces, with none to rescue...'"(John 3:16; Gen 19; Num 16:31-32; Ps 50:22). Moses tells us plainly: "... you will be destroyed for not obeying the Lord your God"(Deut 8:20). This Almighty God declares: "*Obey!*"

Yet His powerful command is then softened by this further scriptural truth: Obedience is bound to love. It is not separate or mutually exclusive. Therefore, because God loves us, He asks us to *obey*. In turn, to love God is to live obediently before Him. And the better we appreciate the tremendous cost of the love and grace we have received from Him, the more compelling our call to the *joy of obeying*!

To answer this call to joy, however, we must first understand and personally accept the preeminent importance of obedience to our spiritual lives. In fact, as Andrew Murray reminds us: "As supreme as is the claim and authority of God is the demand for obedience, as the one thing that is to decide his destiny. In the life of man, to *obey* is the one thing needful."[4] And not only are we called to *obey*, but as disciples of Christ, we are called to pleasure in it (Deut 28:47; Ps 40:8 NLT, ESV). As Oswald Chambers enjoins us: "Simply *obey* Him [God] with unrestrained joy."[5] We are exhorted to joyfully embrace obedience.

The obvious question then becomes: Why? What part does joy have to play in obedience? Does it matter if I pleasure in obeying? Isn't it just important that I do it? And for that matter, is obedience to God relevant at all? As Pharaoh said, "'Who is the Lord,

---

[4] Andrew Murray, *The School of Obedience* (Public Domain).

[5] Oswald Chambers, *My Utmost for His Highest* (Grand Rapids: Discovery House Publishers, 1992), March 28.

that I should *obey* Him…?'"(Ex 5:2). Isn't just being a "good" person good enough?

What evolves in the following pages is an exploration of these questions. It represents my perspectives as a man whose testing in this area compelled me to travel to the center of my being and back again. In that molten core, surrounded by darkness and violent heat, the necessity for obedience once provoked rage. But how like God to transform that liquid fury into new life. Shooting up from my depths, the tumultuous lava of my spiritual interior cooled to form new land. And there, under the brilliance of the heavens, a fruitful place was born. Obedience became a joy.

Like the formation of a volcanic island, finding the joy of obedience in our lives often involves moments of intense spiritual violence and unthinkable power. There is often destruction or fragmentation. For some it is the wrecking ball of grace. For others the refining fire of divine love. For me the shattering of lesser dreams and a trail of transformative ideas hidden in books.

Regardless of the means, however, before we can grasp the *joy of obeying*, disobedience must be broken; for "Disobedience is the root of all sin and misery."[6] From the raw materials that remain after this divine rending, God's transforming power can then create something beautifully new. As Isaiah says, He will bestow upon us a "crown of beauty instead of ashes, the oil of joy instead of mourning, and a garment of praise instead of despair"(Is 61:3).

Sometimes this transforming power comes to us through the words we read. Francois Mauriac, the Nobel Laureate, once said, "A book sometimes turns a

---

[6] Andrew Murray, *The School of Obedience* (Public Domain).

man's life upside down...."⁷ My own understanding of obedience endured this transformative upheaval through a mere few sentences penned by C.S. Lewis. In his imaginative, Venus-like landscape of Perelandra, Lewis describes a temptation scene that brilliantly frames God's heart for obedience in our lives. Lewis challenges us by saying: "What you call obeying Him [God] is but doing what seems good in your own eyes also." He continues: "Is love content with that? You do them [God's commands]...because they are His will, but not only because they are His will. Where can you taste the *joy of obeying* unless He bids you do something for which His bidding is the only reason?"⁸

As I considered the Lord's bidding as the only reason for obeying, my understanding of obedience transformed from an act of compulsion to a willing expression of devotion. I smiled as I "tasted" the *joy of obeying*. For the first time, I saw obedience framed in love.

Love is the beginning and end of the exploration of obedience. In its most simple essence, the *joy of obeying* unveils the language of love. It is the narrative of hearts that hunger after the God they adore.

To propel and fortify this love, there are other powerful and necessary forces that cause us to *obey*: First, the primal motivators, blessing and fear. Then we are aided by the "teachers" who show us *how* to *obey*: pain, shame, and moral obligation (duty). And finally, we have the scriptural reminders of God's roles as

---

⁷ Francois Mauriac, *The Desert of Love* in *A Mauriac Reader* (New York: Farrar, Straus and Giroux, 1968), 210.

⁸ C.S. Lewis, *Perelandra* in *The Space Trilogy* (London: HarperCollins, 2013), 249.

King, Judge, and Creator that command and inspire in us a worship which helps explain *why* we *obey*.

These forces exist because our love is imperfect. Where it sometimes grows cold, these ancillary powers must be engaged to fuel our lackluster efforts to *obey*. While we will explore each of these accessory motivators, in the end, the only obedience that persists, that brings us to joy and carries us all the way home, is the obedience of love.

With obedience springing from love as the end goal, what follows is my effort to refocus and rejuvenate our contemporary understanding of Christian obedience. This endeavor roots itself in the recognition that we now live in a world much like the Church in Ephesus: It has predominately forsaken its first love (Rev 2:4).

But into this contemporary antipathy, I want to tell a love story. I desire to invigorate one of the oldest, and largely unsung, narratives of devotion. In the process, I aim to elevate our conception of obeying from our onerous duty to the joyful privilege of the beloved.

God transformed me in this very way. Where I once dreaded obedience and railed against the God who demanded it of me, I now pleasure in the opportunity to perform those acts that draw me closer to the One who loves me. While I rejoice in the grace that saves and sustains me, I also recognize that only obedience can unlock the fullness of the life Christ calls us to. Only obedience can empower us to claim the eternity He has promised.

My hope is that this book will similarly inspire you to find the life-giving *joy of obeying*. If you do, you will never be the same. Your heart will long to bring a smile to the face of the One you love through the unconditional, absolute obedience of your life.

1.

The Promise of Blessing

The godly are showered with blessings....
—Proverbs 10:6 NLT

Blessed...are those who hear the word of God and obey it.
—Luke 11:28

The first tender green shoots of obedience often spring towards the warm promises of blessing. Even our children and pets recognize a "prize" as perhaps the most attractive reason to *obey*. As my niece readily pointed out, on a primal level we often *obey*, "Because if I do it [*obey*], I might get something good."

When there is potential reward, the goals of obedience may appear to align with our personal interests. In such cases, it takes relatively little effort to *obey*. To these moments, C.S. Lewis pithily says, "What you call obeying...is but doing what seems good in your own eyes also."[9] This form of obedience often appears in familiar and concrete arenas like work and family life.

But what if the rewards for our obedience are more abstract? Will we willingly *obey* if the promised "blessings" are intangible things—like peace and joy (1 Pet 1:2; 2 Chron 30:26)—offered by unseen hands? Is obedience still worth the costs if the blessings are not immediate (Hab 2:3)? What if they wait a lifetime to arrive (Rev 22:12)?

---

[9] C.S. Lewis, *Perelandra* in *The Space Trilogy* (London: HarperCollins, 2013), 249.

In our spiritual lives, these questions surround the relationship between blessing and obedience. Regardless of the conclusions we come to, however, let us make no mistake: God's favor is inextricably bound to obedience. And while it might not appear true in any particular decision to *obey*, God wants us to be convinced: The choice for obedience *always* has God's glory and our best interest in mind. Therefore, if we desire a blessed spiritual life, we must *obey*! As Andrew Murray reminds us, "The one thing by which a creature can glorify God, or enjoy His favor and blessing, is obedience."[10]

The writings of the Pentateuch (the first five books of the Bible) repeatedly demonstrate this truth. Moses says, "The Lord commanded us to *obey*…and to fear the Lord our God, so that we might always prosper and be kept alive….And if we are careful to *obey*…as He commanded…that will be our righteousness"(Deut 6:24-25). In another place, God promises the blessing of His presence in the lives of the obedient: "I will walk among you and be your God, and you will be my people…[enabled] to walk with heads held high"(Lev 26: 12-13).

Perhaps the most focused examination of "Blessings for Obedience" is found in the 28th chapter of Deuteronomy. Shortly before he turns over leadership to Joshua, Moses tells the people:

> If you fully *obey* the Lord your God and carefully follow all His commands I give you today, the Lord your God will set you high above the nations on earth. All these blessings will come upon you and accompany you if you *obey* the Lord your God: You will be blessed in the city

---

[10] Andrew Murray, *The School of Obedience* (Public Domain).

> and blessed in the country. The fruit of your womb will be blessed, and the crops of your land and the young of your livestock....
> Your basket and your kneading trough will be blessed. You will be blessed when you come in and blessed when you go out (v.1-6).

In subsequent verses, Moses then goes on to describe the extension of God's blessing to the defeat of enemies, vocational activities, and even the weather (v. 7-8, 12). In short, he describes a divine blessing that extends to every corner of the obedient life. The promise for obeying is clear: "The Lord will make you the head, not the tail. If you pay attention to the commands of the Lord your God that I give you this day and carefully follow them, you will always be at the top, never at the bottom"(v. 13).

Scripture promises the obedient life will be blessed! To illustrate the direct link between blessing and obedience, the people of Israel had only to look to their forefather Abraham. When God called Abram (yet to be renamed Abraham) to leave his country and go to a new land, God promised him blessing. God said, "'I will make you into a great nation and I will bless you; I will make your name great, and you will be a blessing. I will bless you, and whoever curses you I will curse; and all people of the earth will be blessed through you'"(Gen 12:2-3).

Abram was given the choice to *obey* in faith. But, he certainly did not have to *obey* without the promise of blessing! God repeated it four times in as many sentences. And most importantly, God subsequently fulfilled His promises to Abraham. He is blessed with wealth, power, and a son who will help father the future nation of Israel.

Other examples of specific blessing in the lives of God's faithful are scattered throughout the Old Testament. We see the walls of Jericho collapsing before Joshua simply because he, and the people of Israel, obeyed the seemingly inane command to march around the city walls seven days in a row (Josh 6). There is Gideon, who believed it best to attack the Midianites with an army of thousands. But when God said, "'You have too many men…,'" Gideon obeyed the Lord's command to narrow that number down to 300. The result of this obedience: Midian was destroyed (Judg 7).

Even obedience that sometimes comes reluctantly can be followed by blessing. Naaman, the commander of the army of Aram, was afflicted with leprosy. When he comes to be healed by Elisha, the prophet tells Naaman to go wash in the Jordan River. At first, Naaman refuses. He thinks the miracle should be preceded by more pomp and circumstance. But when Naaman's servant ultimately convinces the commander to grudgingly *obey*, healing comes. Naaman is blessed despite his lackluster obedience (2 Kings 5). His example ought to encourage every one of us who sometimes struggles with the will to *obey*.

In these difficult times, we may doubt not only the process, but also the measure of the blessing we are promised. These moments should be instructed by the example of Jabez. Jabez was "honorable" and remembered in the Chronicles as a man who had the temerity to ask for God's abundance. He cries out to God, "Oh, that you would bless me and enlarge my territory! Let your hand be with me…"(1 Chron 4:10). We are then told, "God granted his request"(v. 10). It may be that we do not receive the fullness of God's blessing because we do not ask like Jabez did. Or, we may be asking in a spirit of disbelief. The Apostle

James reminds us these kinds of requests will not be granted (Jam 1:6-7). But, when we do ask in confident belief, and then live obediently, God says: "Test me in this…and see if I will not throw open the floodgates of heaven and pour out so much blessing that you will not have room enough for it"(Mal 3:10).

Importantly, this promise of blessing is not merely linked to an adherence to the law of the Old Testament. Some of Scripture's greatest examples of blessing due to obedience surface in the New Testament writings. Mary ushers in this New Covenant blessing in obedience. The angel Gabriel is sent to Mary, who is, at the time, probably no more than a child. The angel's first words to Mary indicate God's favor upon her obedient life: "Greetings, you who are highly favored! The Lord is with you"(Luke 1:28). Gabriel then proceeds to tell Mary what God requires of her—to bear the "Son of the Most High"(v. 32).

Mary might have objected to this revelation and ensuing command. She could have attempted to resist, to run, or even, tragically, to end the life God had decided to plant within her. But, we see no willful disobedience in Mary. Despite being asked to do the unimaginable, she decides to believe what she is told. She decides to submit to God's will and *obey* (Luke 1:38). Her actions perfectly demonstrate Andrew Murray's observation on blessing: "The condition for obtaining God's full blessing is *absolute surrender* to Him."[11]

Absolute surrender not only bears fruit in the obedient heart, but also blesses others. Mary's cousin Elizabeth recognizes the result of absolute surrender and says, "'Blessed are you among women and blessed is the child that you will bear!"(Luke 1:42). Later, she

---

[11] Andrew Murray, *Absolute Surrender* (Public Domain).

follows, "'Blessed is she who has believed that what the Lord has said to her will be accomplished!'"(v. 45). Even Mary herself is caused to see the blessed result of her obedience. Mary says, "'From now on all generations will call me blessed, for the Mighty One has done great things for me—holy is His name'"(Luke 1:48-49).

Mary's example further highlights for us this truth: The blessings of obedience are rooted in belief. Other examples in the New Testament make this clear. Two blind men approach Jesus and cry out, "'Have mercy on us, Son of David!'" Jesus responds, "Do you believe I am able to do this?" When the blind men say, "Yes," they are healed. Blessing follows on the heels of their obedient belief (Matt 9:27-29).

Similar favor falls upon the centurion. He approaches Christ with the desire to see his son healed. Jesus says to him, "'Go! It will be done just as you believed it would.'" The centurion *obeys* Jesus' command and leaves for home. He subsequently finds his son healed at the very moment of his obedience (Matt 8:5-13).

A parallel story involves the daughter of Jairus. The girl is ill, and as Jesus is on His way to see her, she dies. But Christ says, "'Don't be afraid; just believe, and she will be healed.'" Jesus commands belief. Healing follows (Luke 8:49-56).

To reinforce the role belief has in garnering the blessings of obedience, Jesus tells us: "'For my Father's will is that everyone who looks to the Son and believes in Him shall have eternal life, and I will raise him up at the last day'"(John 6:40). The Apostle John follows by saying, "And this is His [God's] command: to believe in the name of His Son, Jesus Christ, and to love one another as He commanded us. Those who *obey* His commands live in Him, and He in them"(1 John 3:23-24).

In our obedience to the Lord, we dwell in God, and He dwells in us. We live in Him as we walk as Jesus walked (1 John 2:6). We have ongoing relationship with our Father as we *obey* Him in all things, at all times—*unconditionally,* on the heels of *absolute surrender.* And there, in this place of "unconditional obedience,"[12] our relationship with the Lord will then go on to bear the fruit of blessing.

But what happens when we choose to disobey? Will our lives still bear the fruit of God's blessing? Israel's saga illustrates both the blessings for obedience and the consequences of disobedience. Scripture tells us: Disobedience will be cursed.

The Lord says through Moses, "See, I am setting before you today a *blessing and a curse*—the blessing if you *obey* the commands of the Lord your God that I am giving you today; the curse if you disobey the commands of the Lord your God…"(Deut 11:26-27). The disobedient can look forward to "curses, confusion and rebuke in everything [they] put [their] hand to, until [they] are destroyed and come to sudden ruin…"(Deut 28:20).

This withdrawal of blessing as a result of disobedience vividly appears in the life of Cain. Cain was the son of Adam, and the brother of the righteous man Abel. When God's favor is expressed upon the life of Abel, Cain becomes jealous. In this jealousy, Cain kills his brother. When God then reproaches Cain for this sin, He says to him, "'Your brother's blood cries out to me from the ground. Now you are under a curse and driven from the ground, which opened its mouth to receive your brother's blood from your hand. When you work the ground, it will no longer yield crops for

---

[12] Soren Kierkegaard, *The Lily of the Field and the Bird of the Air* (Princeton: Princeton University Press, 2016), 45.

you. You will be a restless wanderer on earth'"(Gen 4:10-12).

Like Cain, King Saul is another compelling example of the withdrawal of blessing from the life of the disobedient. On two separate occasions, Saul blatantly disobeys the commands God speaks to him through the prophet Samuel. Prior to these failures, however, Saul was the favored son of Israel. He was selected by God to be the first king of His people. The Lord gave Saul power, wealth, and victory over his enemies.

But in this blessing, Saul became proud. Like the people of Israel after him, Hosea's words rang true in Saul's life: "When I [God] fed them, they were satisfied; when they were satisfied they became proud; then they forgot me"(Hosea 13:6). Rather than *obey* God, Saul's pride led him to do what was right in his own eyes.

On one such occasion, Saul is mustering his men for battle at Michmash. The prophet Samuel tells Saul to wait seven days for him to arrive and perform the appropriate sacrifice before battle. Saul, worried over Samuel's apparent tardiness, takes matters into his own hands. He performs the sacrifice himself. To this disobedience, Samuel says, "'You acted foolishly.'" He goes on, "'You have not kept the command the Lord your God gave you; if you had, He would have established your kingdom over Israel for all time. But now your kingdom will not endure...'"(1 Sam 13:13-14).

If we think this judgement too severe, its justice is later confirmed by Saul's repeated and direct disobedience of God's subsequent commands. God tells Saul to destroy the Amalekites, along with all their possessions. Saul proceeds to destroy the army, but then decides to spare King Agag and the "best of the sheep and cattle, the fat calves and lambs—everything that was good"(1 Sam 15:9).

As if aware of his selective adherence to God's commands, Saul then tries to hide his disobedience by telling Samuel, "'I have carried out the Lord's instructions'"(v. 13). But Samuel is not fooled. He responds, "'Why did you not *obey* the Lord? Why did you pounce on the plunder and do evil in the eyes of the Lord?'"(v. 19). Dismissing Saul's excuses about presenting gifts to God, Samuel reminds Saul and us all: "'Does the Lord delight in burnt offerings and sacrifices as much as in obeying the voice of the Lord? To *obey* is better than sacrifice, and to heed is better than the fat of rams. For rebellion is like the sin of divination, and arrogance like the evil of idolatry. Because you have rejected the word of the Lord, He has rejected you as king'"(v. 22-23).

As both Saul and Cain demonstrate, the disobedient life will be cursed. Conversely, as Gideon, Jabez, Mary and others remind us, obeying God positions us to receive His blessings. For God's message to us in Scripture is clear: Spiritual blessing is inextricably bound to obedience. In the words of Andrew Murray, "Obedience is fellowship with God in His will; without it there is not the capacity for seeing and claiming and holding the blessings He has for us."[13] However, "when we deliberately choose to *obey* Him, He will reach to the remotest star and to the ends of the earth to assist us with all of His almighty power."[14] In this hope, let us embrace the *joy of obeying!*

---

[13] Andrew Murray, *The School of Obedience* (Public Domain).

[14] Oswald Chambers, *My Utmost for His Highest* (Grand Rapids: Discovery House, 1992), December 1.

2.

Fear: Standing in Awe

The fear of the Lord is the beginning of wisdom....
—Proverbs 9:10

Blessed is the man who always fears the Lord....
—Proverbs 28:14

Where the promises of blessing fail to inspire and power our obedience, a fear of God and His curse on willful disobedience may move us. Indeed, fear has always been one of the most powerful motivating forces of human behavior. Whether in our parent-child interactions or amidst the whizzing of bullets on the battlefield, fear is capable of inspiring obedience or, at times, even saving our lives through a heightened awareness.

Regrettably, however, "fear" has been almost universally demonized by contemporary culture. Pundits tell parents they need to negotiate and reason with children, rather than instill in them a healthy sense of fear through discipline. Contemporary music similarly sings against fear saying, "Fear Has No Place Here."[15]

But does fear truly have no place in our everyday lives? Is there a role for fear in our spirituality? Is fear necessary to embrace the *joy of obeying*?

The Bible speaks to these questions. In Scripture, we see "fear" weaving its way throughout both the Old and New Testaments. But to understand

---

[15] Ken Stead, "Fear Has No Place Here," *Fear Has No Place Here,* 2015.

its scriptural importance, we must distinguish between *fear*, as it relates to punishment; and *fear*, as in awe or respect.

Looking first to "fear" as it relates to the idea of punishment or consequences, Scripture tells us fear was born on the heels of original sin. After eating the forbidden fruit, Adam hides from God. He says to the Lord, "I heard you in the garden, and I was afraid..." (Gen 3:10). Before the first couple disobeyed, fear did not exist. But in the wake of disobedience, it emerged as the child of sin.

As a direct result of sin's emergence, fear of God's punishment then followed the Lord's people out of Eden. Even some of God's most holy men felt fear because of their sinfulness before a holy God. David says to the Lord, "My flesh trembles in fear of you..."(Ps 119:120). The Apostle Paul describes himself as a servant of God who carried out his ministry with "fear, and with much trembling"(1 Cor 2:3). Both David and Paul trembled with the awareness of God's holiness and its sometimes punishing demand for obedience.

Moses also knew a trembling fear in the presence of God. After descending the mountain with the Commandments in his hand, he finds God's people prostrated before a golden calf. The blatant sins of the people cause Moses to fear the anger of God. He says, "I feared the anger and wrath of the Lord, for He was angry enough with you to destroy you"(Deut 9:19).

Like David and Paul, Moses' fear was also rooted in a personal knowledge of God and His power. Moses witnessed the plagues of Egypt, the parting of the Red Sea, and the burning bush. He knew his God was a "consuming fire"(Deut 4:24). As the writer of Hebrews goes on to remind us, "For we know Him who said, 'It is mine to avenge; I will repay,' and again,

'The Lord will judge His people.' It is a dreadful thing to fall into the hands of the living God"(Heb 10:30-31). Moses knew this "living God" and feared Him.

But did this fear of God's punishing anger cause Moses to love God any less? Arguably, quite the opposite. Indeed, fear of God's powerful anger engendered in Moses the second sense of fear: a holy fear (reverence) of God. In this reverential fear, Moses then instructs God's people: "…what does the Lord your God ask of you but to fear the Lord your God, to walk in all His ways, to love Him…?"(Deut 10:12). Because God was powerful enough to be revered, Moses loved Him with a reverential and obedient fear (Deut 13:4).

A similar composite of fears can be readily seen in the life of Noah. We are told in Hebrews that Noah, "when warned about things not yet seen, in holy fear built an ark to save his family"(11:7). You can be sure Noah feared the destructive power of God when he was told that the Lord was going to destroy the world. Anything less would have been spiritually "irrational" for a man of faith. And this fear of God's punishment on the world's sin then induced a holy fear of reverent submission. The result: Noah obeyed by building an ark.

In the examples of Moses and Noah, we see the subtle transition of fear's role in our spiritual lives. In the beginning, fear may be largely rooted in potential punishment. Ultimately, however, this fear leads us to the second sense of biblical fear: reverence or awe. But the two are never truly unbound. A God whom, on some level, we do not fear, as it relates to punishment or an omnipotent anger, is a God of whom it is very difficult to stand in awe and respect. And holy fear, that of reverence, is the backbone of our spiritual lives. Without holy fear, God is not the Lord of our lives. He does not sit on our throne. As a result, we will not likely *obey* His commands.

A translation of this paradigm to our every day lives evidences in parent-child relationships. Children are often reluctant to *obey* parents who wield a discipline devoid of some fear of punishment. A savvy child may even learn to manipulate his parents to his advantage. Disrespect often fosters unruly children whose willfulness may poise them for personal injury or insult to another. As a result, even non-Christians understand that love demands a certain level of fear as it relates to disciplining. The writer of Hebrews reminds us: "…the Lord disciplines those He loves, and He punishes everyone He accepts as a son"(Heb 12:6).

While love is not compatible with revenge or abuse, discipline is an essential component of love. To discipline effectively requires either a position or possession of power in relation to another. The wielding of this power must induce a level of fear if it is to affect our behavior. Between parents and children, the difference may be physical stature or financial resources. But in God's case, it is the difference between an immortal, omnipotent Creator and a willful, finite creation.

The Old Testament gives us countless examples of Israel's disobedience inducing God to discipline His people in love. If we, like the people of Israel, are also objects of God's love, should we therefore expect, or even hope, for anything less from God's love in our own lives? And as this love sometimes chooses to demonstrate its almighty power through discipline, shouldn't we then have some fear of God in our hearts? How can we not, like Moses, tremble in the face of omnipotence? Jeremiah says:

> "Should you not fear me?" declares the Lord. "Should you not tremble in my presence? I made the sand a boundary for the sea, an everlasting barrier it cannot cross....But these people have stubborn hearts; they have turned aside and gone away. They do not say to themselves, 'Let us fear the Lord our God, who gives autumn and spring rains in season, who assures us of the regular weeks of harvest.' Your wrongdoings have kept these away; your sins have deprived you of good (Jer 5:22-25).

As Jeremiah reminds us, we are called to tremble in the presence of Almighty God.

Reiterating this exhortation, Jesus Himself tells us to fear God. He says, "Do not be afraid of those who kill the body but cannot kill the soul. Rather, be afraid of the One who can destroy both body and soul in hell"(Matt 10:28). Elsewhere, He says, "But I will show you whom you should fear: Fear Him who after the killing of the body, has the power to throw you into hell. Yes, I tell you, fear Him"(Luke 12:5). Perhaps to our shame, we are told even the demons understand this and "shudder"(Jam 2:19).

This demonic shuddering, like the trembling of Moses (Heb 12:21), shows us a fear of God which is rooted in both the reality of potential consequences as well as deep awe and respect. To fear the Lord, therefore, is to simultaneously recognize His capacity to destroy us, as well as our need to stand in awe of His glory, power, majesty, and unimaginable love. As God's victorious armies will one day declare, "Who will not fear you, O Lord, and bring glory to your name?"(Rev 15:4).

But how do we then reconcile this rhetorical, coming reality with the Apostle John's famous declaration, "There is no fear in love. But perfect love drives out fear, because fear has to do with punishment. The one who fears is not made perfect in love"(1 John 4:18)? Because love is the driving force of the gospel message, this verse has caused many Christians to disparage fear in their spiritual lives. They may view it as an impediment to knowing God because of the cautious distance created by the potential for discipline. It may be seen as a sign of weakness or cowardice few want to admit. It might be considered an inconsistency in a "loving" relationship between a Father and His devoted children. But must fear embody these negative connotations? Is that the full ken of what John's message intends?

To answer these questions, we must appropriately position our biblical understanding of fear in our lives of faith. John says, "*perfect* love drives out fear, because fear has to do with consequences. The one who fears is not made *perfect* in love"(1 John 4:18). Importantly, John posits fear in relation to "perfection" in love. But are we yet perfect? Or, are we maturing into possession of the perfection Christ has given us? And as we do, what role does fear play in inspiring us to *obey*?

The Apostle Paul speaks to these inquiries by positioning his own life in the spiritual race toward heaven. He says:

> Not that I have already obtained all this, or have already been made perfect, but I press on to take hold of that for which Christ Jesus took hold of me. Brothers, I do not consider myself yet to have taken hold of it. But one thing I do: Forgetting what is behind and straining toward what is ahead, I press on toward the goal to win

the prize for which God has called me
heavenward in Christ Jesus"(Phil 3:12-14).

Paul recognizes he is moving toward the perfection Christ has given him. As the writer of Hebrews says, "by one sacrifice He [God] has made perfect forever those who are being made holy"(Heb 10:14). Amidst this sanctifying process, Paul urges us to "continue to work out [our] salvation with fear and trembling..." (Phil 2:12).

This "work" Paul calls us to is the work of obedience. Until we stand before our Father and claim the perfection given to us in the blood of Jesus, we live in a world dominated by sin. In it, we struggle to *obey*. And as we do, we must maintain some level of fear in our spiritual lives. It helps keep us honest, faithful, and focused.

Holy fear also gives us perspective for all other worldly concerns. When we truly fear God, all other fears fall away. We find the providential perspective that causes us to say, like David, "The Lord is my light and my salvation—whom shall I fear? The Lord is the stronghold of my life—of whom shall I be afraid?"(Ps 27:1). Whether we face war, hardship, famine, or the powers of darkness, holy fear allows us to stand confident in God's grace (Ps 27:3, Rom 8:35, 38). We are convinced: "God is our refuge and strength, an ever-present help in trouble"; therefore, "we will not fear, though the earth give way and the mountains fall into the heart of the sea..."(Ps 46:1-2). We find that we are "more than conquerors through Him who loved us"(Rom 8:37). We are spiritual warriors equipped to *obey* because we fear both God's holiness and His power to affect our lives.

Abraham's life perhaps best demonstrates this power of holy fear. In his journey to Mt. Moriah, he shows us how obedience is linked to holy fear. When Abraham obeyed God's command to sacrifice Isaac, God said to him, "Now I know that you fear God, because you have not withheld from me your son, your only son"(Gen 22:12). When we fear God like Abraham did, we have little trouble obeying. We find the strength to do the seemingly impossible.

As Jesus reminds us, "With God all things are possible"(Matt 19:26). However, only a fear of God in our lives will set the stage for this power of possibility. In our journeys onward toward the perfection Christ has purchased for us, holy fear may often empower our imperfect obedience. Until that day when our imperfect love perfectly joins Love itself, we are wise to see fear as an essential component of God's loving relationship with us.

To say, therefore, that fear has no place in our relationship with God is to believe in a love which minimizes the omnipotence of the God who is Love. His love has no boundaries. In its immensity, it encompasses the polarities of fear—awe for God's majesty and His power to heal and destroy. For this reason, choose to fear a God whose love is great enough to swallow fear itself. In this truth, you will find the *joy of obeying*.

3.

Pain: The Great Teacher

Sometimes it takes a painful experience to make us change our ways.
—Proverbs 20:30 GNT

...He [Christ] humbled Himself and became obedient to death —even death on a cross!
—Philippians 2:8

While blessing and fear are among the most primal motivators of obedience, pain teaches us *how* to *obey*. Perhaps ironically, suffering best points us towards the *joy of obeying*. But finding joy in painful experiences is never easy. Frustrated screams and copious tears often deafen and blind us to everything but our hurt. As C.S. Lewis reminds us, in these moments pain is "unmasked, unmistakeable evil" which "insists upon being attended to." It is "God's megaphone to rouse a deaf world."[16] And whether it assaults the body or the heart and soul, it always leaves scars. If it does not, it is not pain, but rather some effete phantom of the imagination. And though God's grace worked out in the hands of time can heal the pain of our deepest wounds, it does not cause us to completely forget them. The scars fade but do not erase.

But if God truly loves us, why doesn't He expunge the memory of our pain? Why allow pain into our lives at all? In his own attempt to reconcile God's

---

[16] C.S. Lewis, *The Problem of Pain* (New York: HarperCollins, 1996), 90-91.

love with the persistent scars of memory, Soren Kierkegaard says, "But he who loves God has no need of tears…and forgets his suffering in love, indeed forgets so completely that afterwards not the least hint of his pain would remain were God Himself not to remember it; for God sees in secret and knows the distress and counts the tears and forgets nothing."[17] Kierkegaard reminds us God stands with us in our pain: Our scars persist because God's memory is infallible.

Therefore, as He lives in us, some memory of pain always etches our hearts—and rightfully so. These scars bear witness to the time spent in the presence of a great teacher. Even the resurrected Jesus still bore the scars of nail-pierced hands when He appeared before His disciples. His hands and feet were visible witness to an unimaginable pain. And although He needed no reminding of His suffering in obedience to God's will, His disciples did. So do we.

Like the disciples, we will not likely *obey* God, much less come to know Him, without looking to Christ's scars and remembering His pain on Calvary. We will also need to consider our part in His ultimate sacrifice and link our own suffering to our sin. In this contemplation, we might then ask: As followers of a God who loves us enough to die for us, should we expect lives devoid of the pain that also pierces us to the point of scarring? Shall we not say with David, "They have pierced my hands and my feet"(Ps 22:16)? Is it not better to see pain as an essential instrument of a divine love we are meant to embrace?

The spiritually mature know the answer to this question. Indeed, they are convinced: Suffering may be one of God's greatest gifts to us. It is the "necessary evil" on the road to knowing God, to learning the

---

[17] Soren Kierkegaard, *Fear and Trembling* (London: Penguin Books, 2003) 143-144.

obedience He requires of us, and to claiming His eternal blessings in our lives. And while we might wish, like Jabez, for a blessed life "free from pain"(1 Chron 4:10), such a desire, if granted, will limit our ability to truly know and love the God we wish to serve.

Therefore, instead of wishing pain away, we are wiser to first understand pain as God's essential ingredient to know Christ. Thomas Merton says, "The Lord did not create suffering. Pain…came into the world with the fall of man. But after man had chosen suffering in preference to the joys of union with God, the Lord turned suffering itself into a way by which man could come to the perfect knowledge of God."[18]

The Apostle Paul perhaps understood this truth best. He says, "I want to know Christ and the power of His resurrection and the fellowship of sharing in His sufferings, becoming like Him in His death, and so, somehow, to attain to the resurrection of the dead"(Phil 3:10). But to know Christ as Paul desires, we must "*obey* His commands." Indeed, "The man who says, 'I know Him,' but does not do what He commands is a liar, and the truth is not in him"(1 John 2:3-4).

As the Apostles remind us, knowing Christ necessitates obedience. When we know Him, we understand: "Whether in His sufferings on earth or in His glory in heaven, whether in Himself or in us, obedience is what the heart of Christ is set upon."[19]

But we cannot learn to *obey* without pain. God has ordained that pain should be the primary tool in teaching us obedience. Jesus Christ Himself demonstrated this for us: "Although He was a son, He

---

[18] Thomas Merton, *No Man is an Island* (New York: Harcourt, 1983), 89.

[19] Andrew Murray, *The School of Obedience* (Public Domain).

learned obedience from what He suffered and, once made perfect, He became the source of eternal salvation for all who *obey* Him…"(Heb 5:8-9). Our Lord had to "learn" obedience—He had to walk it out. And in so doing, He endured much pain.

In the midst of this pain, Jesus was the suffering servant: "He was despised and rejected by men, a man of sorrows, and familiar with suffering. Like one from whom men hide their faces, He was despised, and we esteemed Him not"(Is 53:3). Isaiah then reminds us that Christ "took up our infirmities and carried our sorrows, yet we considered Him stricken by God, smitten by Him, and afflicted"(v. 4). Jesus was "pierced for our transgressions, He was crushed for our iniquities, and the punishment that brought peace was upon Him"(v. 5). It was, as Isaiah recounts, God's will to "crush Him and cause Him to suffer"(v. 10).

Aware of this predestined pain, Jesus could have resisted His role as the suffering servant. And yet, He decidedly did not. He chose to *obey*. And though we find Him pleading in the Garden of Gethsemane to take the cup of God's wrath away, He immediately submits to God's will, despite the pain. As Andrew Murray reminds us, "Christ needed suffering that in it He might learn to *obey* and give up His will to the Father at any cost….He learned obedience, He became obedient unto death, that He might become the author of our salvation. He became the author of salvation through obedience, that He might save those 'who *obey* Him.'"[20] The Apostle Paul puts it this way: Jesus, "Who being in very nature God…made Himself nothing, taking the very nature of a servant, being made in human likeness…humbled Himself and became

---

[20]Andrew Murray, *The School of Obedience* (Public Domain)

obedient to death—even death on a cross!"(Phil 2:6-8). At every turn, Christ said: "not my will, but yours be done"(Luke 22:42).

With Christ's submission to suffering as our example, we must understand pain as an integral part of Christian obedience. If our Lord suffered to *obey*, we must also: "As obedience was with Him absolutely necessary to procure, it is with us absolutely necessary to inherent salvation."[21] Did Christ not say, "'No servant is greater than his master,'" and "In this world you will have trouble…"(John 15:20, 16:33)? Should we then be surprised at the painful trials that come into our lives, "as though something strange were happening to [us]"(1 Peter 4:12)? Decidedly, no! We must remember: There is no Christ-like obedience that will not cost us something.

We can respond to this reality in one of two ways: rejection or willing submission. The Old Testament is a sinusoidal story of Israel's struggle between these two extremes. Sadly, however, Israel more often than not chose rejection, evident in their constant grumbling against God. In times of difficulty, Israel "grumbled against Moses and Aaron…"(Num 14:2). As a result of this ingratitude and lack of trust, God says: "'How long will this wicked community grumble against me? I have heard the complaints of these grumbling Israelites'"(Num 14:27). In their discontent, an entire generation died in the desert; disobedience and a lack of trust in God's power to conquer the Palestinians kept them from the Promised Land.

Akin to grumbling, rejection of God in the midst of pain can also produce the spirit of bitterness. As Solomon says, "Each heart knows its own bitterness…"(Prov 14:10). Even the faithful Job, of

---

[21] Andrew Murray, *The School of Obedience* (Public Domain).

whom God said, "There is no one on earth like him; he is blameless and upright, a man who fears God and shuns evil"(Job 1:8), found himself guilty of bitterness in the midst of his suffering. Job says, "'Therefore I will not keep silent; I will speak out in the anguish of my spirit, I will complain in the bitterness of my soul'"(Job 7:11). Later he says, "'I loathe my very life; therefore I will give free rein to my complaint and speak out in the bitterness of my soul'"(Job 10:1).

But while Job's bitterness (and perhaps our own) might, on some level, be understandable in view of his horrific pain, Scripture tells us there is no place for it. The writer of Hebrews reminds us: "See to it that no one misses the grace of God and that no bitter root grows up to cause trouble and defile many"(Heb 12:15). Paul says, "Get rid of all bitterness…"(Eph 4:31).

In addition to bitterness, rejection of pain may also produce anger, rage, revenge, or resentment (Eph 4:26, 31). All of these negative emotions evidence our disobedience. And while all of us know moments when our spirits touch these depths, Christ's disciples do not remain there. To wallow in the pit of pain is to "give the devil a foothold" in our lives (Eph 4:27).

For this reason, Christians intent on obedient lives are called to embrace the pain that enters their lives with the perspective of the Holy Spirit. As Thomas Merton reminds us: "Pain does not cease to be pain, but we can be glad of it because it enables Christ to suffer in us and give glory to His Father by being greater, in our hearts, than suffering could ever be."[22] We are encouraged to accept pain as a gift, rather than reject it. We should not seek it out or wish for it. But neither do we abjure pain when God, in His

---

[22] Thomas Merton, *No Man is an Island* (New York: Harcourt, 1983), 90.

providence, brings it into our lives as His refining instrument of love.

In light of His great love for us, we must remember the admonition of C.S. Lewis: "We were made not primarily that we may love God (though we were made for that too) but that God may love us, that we may become objects in which the Divine love may rest 'well pleased'."[23] To become these objects of divine love, we must be transformed. And because God is who is He is, His perfect love for us "must, in the nature of things, be impeded and repelled by certain stains in our present character, and...He must labor to make us lovable."[24] This divine "labor" in our lives almost always involves pain. To go from where we are to where we need to be, we must necessarily endure the sufferings of love.

But when we see pain in light of God's great love for us, everything changes. Although the specific circumstances will still be challenging (sometimes desperately so!), we can learn to see pain as a tool in the shaping hands of a loving Potter who desires to teach us *how* to *obey*. Rather than rejecting pain, we might learn to embrace it. We might even learn to rejoice in it!

The Apostle Peter instructs us in this call to rejoice in suffering. He says, "In this you greatly rejoice, though now for a little while you have had to suffer grief in all kinds of trials. These have come so that your faith—of greater worth than gold, which perishes even though refined by fire—may be proved genuine and may result in praise, glory and honor when Jesus Christ is revealed"(1 Pet 1:6-7). Later he goes on to say,

---

[23] C.S. Lewis, *The Problem of Pain* (New York: HarperCollins, 1996), 41.

[24] 41.

"But rejoice that you participate in the sufferings of Christ, so that you may be overjoyed when His glory is revealed"(1 Pet 4:13).

Paul, the great missionary to the Gentiles, also demonstrates an understanding of Peter's perspective on suffering. He says to the Romans, "Not only so, we also rejoice in our sufferings, because we know that suffering produces perseverance; perseverance, character; and character, hope. And hope does not disappoint us, because God has poured out His love into our hearts by the Holy Spirit…"(Rom 5:3-5).

In the knowledge of God's love for him, Paul rejoiced in the workings of pain in his life. Though he suffered a "thorn in my flesh, a messenger of Satan, to torment me"(2 Cor 12:7), Paul was capable of seeing his thorn as God's instrument of power in his life. True, he pleaded for God to take it away, as we might. But when the Lord allowed it to remain, Paul had the wisdom to rejoice in it. He says, "Therefore, I will boast all the more gladly about my weaknesses, so that Christ's power may rest on me. That is why, for Christ's sake, I delight in weaknesses, in insults, in hardships, in persecutions, in difficulties. For when I am weak, then I am strong"(2 Cor 12: 9-10).

In Christ's strength, Paul stood obedient and resolute in the midst of great pain. He says, "We are hard pressed on every side, but not crushed; perplexed, but not in despair; persecuted, but not abandoned; struck down, but not destroyed"(2 Cor 4:8-9). Paul understood "our present sufferings are not worth comparing with the glory that will be revealed in us" when Christ comes again (Rom 8:18). He was convinced "that in all things God works for the good of those who love Him," and that no "trouble or hardship or persecution or famine or nakedness or danger or sword" could separate him from the love of Christ

(Rom 8:28, 35). With such confidence in Jesus, Paul recognized suffering as an integral part of God's amazing and perfecting love.

Similarly empowered by the Spirit, we, like Peter and Paul before us, are encouraged to see and rejoice in the perfecting role of pain in our spiritual obedience. Therefore, when we encounter suffering, let us consider embracing it as an instructor of obedience rather than rejecting it. Let us dare to place our sufferings in the context of God's love for us and all that He desires to teach us. When we do this, we claim His great blessings in our lives. We stand showered in His love.

In this love, we might then say, like the transformed King David, "Before I was afflicted I went astray, but now I *obey* your word"(Ps 119:67). Despite the scars of our most painful moments, we might have the perspective to declare the blessing of our sufferings: "It was good for me to be afflicted so that I might learn your decrees," and "Surely it was for my benefit that I suffered such anguish"(Ps 119:71; Is 38:17). Ultimately, we might even have the courage to see our pain, as Andrew Murray reminds us, as the only way of identification with Christ, our great example and teacher in obedience: "On earth Christ was a learner in the school of obedience; in heaven He teaches it to His disciples here on earth."[25]

As pupils in His school of obedience, let us dare to see pain as God's teaching instrument of love.

---

[25]Andrew Murray, *The School of Obedience* (Public Domain)

4.

Shame: The Voice of the Godly Conscience

Sin and shame go together. Lose your honor, and you will get scorn in its place.
—*Proverbs 18:3 GNT*

Some of our most painful life experiences result from disobedience. Disobedience to God then births shame (or at least it should). But while our shameful disobedience deserves God's curse, we have been rescued by His love instead. And in this redeeming love, shame, like pain, has been reclaimed and repurposed as one of the Spirit's tools in teaching us *how* to *obey*.

Yet despite this divine refiguring of shame for our spiritual growth, the contemporary western world seeks to eliminate the concept of shame altogether. Some counselors universally label it as "unhealthy," while Hollywood devalues it to the point of meaninglessness. In television series like *Shameless*, we see previously taboo topics like premarital sex, substance abuse, homosexuality, abortion, and others, vividly and flamboyantly explored. These media expressions of "shamelessness" embody what C.S. Lewis describes as the culture's new dogma: "We are told to 'get things out in the open,' not for the sake of self-humiliation, but on the grounds that these 'things' are very natural and we need not be ashamed of them."[26] Our culture pleasures in unbridled "pleasuring."

But while the public increasingly celebrates the "shameless" life, are we truly to believe there is no longer anything to be ashamed of? Is shame merely a

---

[26] C.S. Lewis, *The Problem of Pain* (New York: HarperCollins, 1996), 50.

restrictive, repressive "evil" that is to be looked at with contempt and eradicated from our lives? Or, does shame have a proper place in our spirituality? Is it an essential component to living obediently before God?

Disobedience and shame have been linked since the very beginning. Perhaps ironically, today's "shameless" culture is, in a perverse and addled way, longing for the "Edenic" world it left behind. As Dietrich Bonhoeffer explains, "Shame is man's ineffaceable recollection of his estrangement from the origin; it is grief for this estrangement, and the powerless longing to return to unity with the origin."[27] In Eden, man and woman were created in a holy shamelessness. Adam was made in God's "own image"(Gen 1:27). Eve was then formed from Adam's flesh (2:23). Together, "The man and the woman were both naked, and they felt no shame"(2:25). They were in unity with God.

But this blissful absence of shame was short-lived. It depended upon a bond of obedience that humankind broke. God said to Adam, "'You are free to eat from any tree in the garden; but you must not eat from the tree of the knowledge of good and evil, for when you eat of it you will surely die'"(Gen 2:16-17). No sooner had Eve and Adam disobeyed this command, than shame entered the world. The eyes of the first couple opened, and they "realized that they were naked; so they sewed fig leaves together and made coverings for themselves"(3:7). In the shame of their disobedience, they then hid from God. Just as sin birthed fear into the world, it also birthed shame.

Because of this initial and direct relationship with sin, shame then became associated with the sordid, unrespectable, and disgraceful. It represented disunion

---

[27] Dietrich Bonhoeffer, *Ethics* (New York: Simon & Schuster, 1995), 24.

with God.[28] Estrangement from the Creator ensued. And in this growing distance, shame became the antithesis of not only union with God, but also of honor and glory.

As a result of this moral dipole, the early eastern world subsequently developed societies based on the tension between honor and shame. Remnants of these societies persist today. And because these sociological traces are woven into current thinking, understanding the role of biblical shame and its proper place in our spiritual lives of obedience necessitates an appreciation of this powerful honor and shame relationship.

One of the places in Scripture where this relationship appears most pronounced is the Psalms. The Psalter is punctuated with evidence that shame is associated with the disgraced spiritual state of disobedience. It is a place David does not want to be in. He abhors estrangement from the God he loves. So he cries out: "Do not let me be put to shame, nor let my enemies triumph over me. No one whose hope is in you will ever be put to shame, but they will be put to shame who are treacherous without excuse"(Ps 25:2-3). He says in another place, "In you, O Lord, I have taken refuge; let me never be put to shame"(Ps 71:1). The place of honor, in David's eyes, rests with God's favor: "Those who look to Him are radiant; their faces are never covered with shame"(Ps 34:5).

Just as the absence of shame denotes favorable standing with God, so the presence of shame follows God's enemies. Indeed, David repeatedly wishes disgrace and shame upon his enemies. He says, "May those who seek my life be disgraced and put to shame"(Ps 35:4). Later, David says, "May all who seek

---

[28] Dietrich Bonhoeffer, *Ethics* (New York: Simon & Schuster, 1995). 25.

to take my life be put to shame and confusion; may all who desire my ruin be turned back in disgrace"(Ps 40:14). And then yet again: "May my accusers perish in shame; may those who want to harm me be covered with scorn and disgrace"(Ps 71:13). Clearly, David sees shame as an "evil" perfectly fit for his enemies.

But perhaps the Psalter's best contribution to our understanding of shame is its beautiful embodiment of the moral conscience behind obedience. David repeatedly pours out his heart to God in all seasons of the soul, including his moments of shame. In Psalm 51, David's sense of shame causes him to cry out to God for mercy. He has sinned before God and he knows it. David says, "Against you, you only, have I sinned, and done what is evil in your sight"(v. 4). Filled with an estranging shame, he longs to be united with his God. He pleads: "Hide your face from my sins...," and "Do not cast me from your presence or take your Holy Spirit from me"(v. 9, 11).

Such entreaties demonstrate the first principle of *godly* shame: it is the sign that the Holy Spirit resides in the soul. As Andrew Murray reminds us, "The Holy Spirit speaks through conscience."[29] It is the main medium of His expression in our lives. This is only true, however, as we abide in Christ. Ironically, if we do not remain in Him, conscience, as Bonhoeffer notes, "is the sign of man's disunion with himself."[30] The Apostle Paul sums up this pairing when he says, "To the pure all things are pure, but to those who are corrupted and do not believe, nothing is pure. In fact, both their minds and consciences are corrupt. They claim to know God, but by their actions they deny Him. They

---

[29] Andrew Murray, *The School of Obedience* (Public Domain)

[30] Dietrich Bonhoeffer, *Ethics* (New York: Simon & Schuster, 1995), 27.

are detestable, disobedient and unfit for doing anything good"(Titus 1:15-16).

But in the purity of the Spirit, shame is divine communication. When spiritually healthy Christians sin against God as David did, and then feel ashamed, they can be sure the Holy Spirit is living in them and speaking. For as Andrew Murray notes, "a good conscience is complete obedience to God day by day...."[31] Therefore, when we disobey God and sin, our consciences alert us to the Holy Spirit's grieving within us (Eph 4:30). That alert is shame.

Obversely, the absence of shame in the presence of sin indicates spiritual death. As the prophet Zephaniah says, "the unrighteous know no shame"(Zeph 3:5). Jeremiah comments similarly: "Are they ashamed of their loathsome conduct? No, they have no shame at all; they do not even know how to blush"(Jer 6:15).

For this reason, God's people always maintain the capacity for the spiritual "blush." Sensitized by the indwelling Holy Spirit, Christians recognize shame as one of God's instruments to draw us back to Him and to help us *obey*. In this Spirit, the prophet Jeremiah has no trouble owning the shame of sin in his life. He says, "Let us lie down in our shame, and let our disgrace cover us. We have sinned against the Lord our God, both we and our fathers, from our youth till this day we have not obeyed the Lord our God"(Jer 3:25).

Likewise, Daniel, another man filled with God's Spirit, says, "O Lord, we and our kings, our princes and our fathers are covered with shame because we have sinned against you." Further, he says, "We have not obeyed the Lord our God or kept the laws He gave us through His servants the prophets. All Israel has

---

[31] Andrew Murray, *Absolute Surrender* (Public Domain).

transgressed your law and turned away, refusing to *obey* you"(Dan 9:8, 10-11).

As both these prophets suggest, shame is the appropriate response for the sin and disobedience of our lives. C.S. Lewis echoes this when he says, "But unless Christianity is wholly false, the perception of ourselves which we have in moments of shame must be the only true one; and even Pagan society has usually recognized 'shamelessness' as the nadir of the soul."[32] We are not to be consumed by shame, and so fall into Satan's traps of false humility, self-obsession, or a spiritual depression fatally distancing us from the God who loves us and longs to heal us. But, neither are we to eschew shame as an irrelevant and restrictive moral nuisance.

Rather, we do best to see shame as a teacher and guide to godly obedience. Shame focuses where we have not obeyed and brings us to the forgiveness of Christ. And, as Dante reminds us from the depths of the Inferno, "shame, which makes a servant—in his kind lord's presence—brave," may then encourage and propel us to *obey*.[33]

David, perhaps, does the finest job of expressing shame's motive force for obedience in our lives. In Psalm 119, he recognizes the power of obedience to prevent shame. He further describes how shame impels our efforts to *obey*. He says, "Oh, that my ways were steadfast in obeying your decrees! Then I would not be put to shame when I consider all your commands"(v. 5-6). He goes on to say, "I hold fast to your statues, O Lord; do not let me be put to shame"(v. 31). In his will to *obey*, David prays: "May my heart be

---

[32]C.S. Lewis, *The Problem of Pain* (New York: HarperCollins, 1996), 50.

[33] Dante Alighieri, *Inferno,* XVII:89-90 (Public Domain).

blameless toward your decrees, that I may not be put to shame"(v. 80).

But even when we do sin and find ourselves feeling rightly ashamed, Scripture gives us hope. We are not eternal prisoners to our shame. The Apostle Paul speaks to this hope when he quotes Isaiah: "As it is written: 'See I lay in Zion a stone that causes men to stumble and a rock that makes them fall, and the one who trusts in Him will never be put to shame'"(Rom 9:33). Indeed, one day, through the work of Christ, we will be completely restored to our place of *godly* "shamelessness." We will once more be unified with the Lord. The Spirit living in us anticipates this day as "we groan, longing to be clothed with our heavenly dwelling, because when we are clothed we will not be found naked"(2 Cor 5:2-3). As Bonhoeffer says, "Shame can be overcome only when the original unity is restored, when man is once again clothed by God...."[34] Until this unification, shame serves as an agent of godly obedience.

As we look forward to the triumphal day when unity with God will be restored, Isaiah's words fill us with hope: "Do not be afraid; you will not suffer shame. Do not fear disgrace; you will not be humiliated. You will forget the shame of your youth…"(Is 54:4). Later, the prophet goes on to say, "Instead of their shame, my people will receive a double portion, and instead of disgrace they will rejoice in their inheritance; and so they will inherit a double portion in their land, and everlasting joy will be theirs"(Is 61:7).

However, until this moment of final restoration —when honor is restored and we stand with "an eternal weight of glory beyond all comparison"(2 Cor 4:17 ESV)—shame has an essential role to play in the

---

[34]Dietrich Bonhoeffer, *Ethics* (New York: Simon & Schuster, 1995), 27.

life of spiritual obedience. Shame focuses our disobedience and propels us towards the redeeming love of Christ. In contrast, our society's current efforts to annihilate shame position us for spiritual ruination. As C.S. Lewis reminds us: "In trying to extirpate shame we have broken down one of the ramparts of the human spirit...." We, like the Trojans dragging the horse into our city, are on the brink of destruction.[35] But let us not be misled: "'Bad company corrupts good character'"(1 Cor 15:33). To these self-injurious efforts, the Apostle Paul says, "Come back to your senses as you ought, and stop sinning; for there are some who are ignorant of God—I say this to your shame"(1 Cor 15:34).

Paul's exhortation may sound ruthlessly hard, but he desires us to feel shame as God intends: a temporary and redeeming gift of the pure conscience, granted to help guide us to obedience in our homeward journeys into the arms of a Father who will one day wipe away all shame. The good news is that the fruit of our obedience will fulfill what Isaiah promises: "The Sovereign Lord will wipe away the tears from all faces; he will remove the disgrace of His people from all the earth. The Lord has spoken"(Is 25:8).

---

[35]C.S. Lewis, *The Problem of Pain* (New York: HarperCollins, 1996), 50.

5.

Duty: Moral Obligation

Fear God and keep His commandments, for this is the whole duty of man.
—Ecclesiastes 12:13

Sometimes simply obeying by doing our "duty" is the best way to avoid the humiliation of shame. And while duty may appear a long way from joy, just fulfilling obligations often teaches us the spiritual disciplines required to embrace the *joy of obeying*.

But what is "duty" when it appears to have so many "faces" in our everyday lives? It can be seen in our responsibilities at work, our expected activities or roles in our families, and even in our moral thinking and ensuing conduct. Despite its multiplicity of "selves," however, one commonality emerges: we often associate duty with obligation. In our minds, it is seen as an obedience to someone or something. It is perceived as a thing we have to do—like it or not.

Often, this sense of compulsion results in a negative connotation. We might even catch ourselves blaming God for our sense of duty, saying, "If you made me, you made this feeling of responsibility that I've always carried about like a sack of bricks." [36] Sometimes, however, we have the wisdom to recognize the purpose and privilege of our call to the duty of obedience.

The biblical presentation of "duty" encompasses this full range of human understanding. Much

---

[36]Graham Greene, *The Heart of the Matter* (New York: Penguin Books, 1999), 230.

of the Old Testament focuses on man's duty to *obey* the laws of God and to fulfill the roles He has given the members of the Israelite community. Whether it is in the care of the Tent of Meeting, the sacrifices before God, or the treatment of orphans and widows, the Old Testament specifically delineates duties to the Israelites. Similarly, the New Testament also speaks of duty, largely within the contextual role of "servant." Together, within these two Covenants, duty's appeal extends to God's prophets, kings, priests, and every Israelite and Gentile in between—even you and me.

But in what ways is the scriptural sense of duty specifically related to our call to *obey*? And what duties, if any, does the contemporary Christian have to the God of the Bible? How do we reconcile these "duties" with King Solomon's exhortation: "Fear God and keep His commandments, for this is the full duty of man"(Ecc 12:13)?

One of the overarching paradigms within which the Bible explores this "duty" to God is the relationship of servant to master. Most of Scripture's godly men and women clearly understood their roles as "servant" or "bondservant"(slave) before a Divine Master. When Abraham is visited by the Lord, the father of Israel says, "'If I have found favor in your eyes...do not pass your servant by'"(Gen 18:3). Moses, the prophet and great scribe of God's Law, is described at his death as "the servant of the Lord"(Deut 34:5). The priest and prophet Samuel cries out to God: "'Speak, for your servant is listening'"(1 Sam 3:10). And Job, the "blameless and upright man...who fears God and shuns evil," is affectionately described by God as "servant"(Job 1:8).

The godly kings of Israel also understood their roles as servants of the Lord. After the prophet Nathan promises God's blessing over his life, King

David prays to God. He says, "'What more can David say to you for honoring your servant? For you know your servant, O Lord. For the sake of your servant and according to your will, you have done this great thing and made known all these great promises. There is no one like you, O Lord...'"(1 Chron 17:18-20).

David's son King Solomon also recognizes his role as a servant who must carry out the "duties" of the Lord. At the beginning of his reign, Solomon prays to the Lord. He says, "'Now, O Lord my God, you have made your servant king in place of my father David. But I am only a little child and do not know how to carry out my duties'"(1 Kings 3:7). He continues: "So give your servant a discerning heart to govern your people and to distinguish between right and wrong"(1 Kings 3:9). In this prayer, Solomon articulates a clear understanding of his servanthood and his ensuing duty to *obey*.

But there is, perhaps, no more focused biblical examination of the "servant's" duty to *obey* than Psalm 119. In this longest of the Psalms, the writer (probably King David) persistently marries the image of servant with the subsequent need to *obey*. He says, "Do good to your servant, and I will live; I will *obey* your word"(v.17). David goes on to use the word "*obey*" twenty times in the remainder of the psalm. Numerous synonyms then repeatedly reinforce this idea. His specific concern appears to be the importance of obeying God's commands: the "law of the Lord"(v. 1). He thematically begins the psalm saying, "You [God] have laid down precepts that are to be fully obeyed"(v. 4).

Reiterations of this duty are then declared throughout the psalm. There is an almost overwhelming sense of personal conviction to ensure obedience is fulfilled. David says: "I will *obey* your decrees"; "I will *obey* your word"; "I will always *obey* your law..."; "I *obey* your precepts"; "I will hasten and not delay to *obey* your commands"; "I will *obey* the statues of your mouth"(v. 8, 17, 44, 56, 60, 88). Clearly, David recognizes the importance of obedience and possesses the faithful servant's determination to see it through.

This determination, however, is then coupled with a wisdom and humility that recognizes its dependence on the Master it seeks to *obey*. In fulfilling his duty, David implores God for help. He says things like: "Keep me from deceitful ways"; "Teach me, O Lord, to follow your decrees"; "Turn my heart towards your statues…"; "Turn my eyes away from worthless things"; "You are my refuge and my shield"(v. 29, 33, 36-37, 114).

The teachable spirit expressed in these verses then further defines our duty to *obey* by presenting its foil: *disobedience*. He says, "All the wicked of the earth you discard like dross; therefore I love your statues"(v. 119). In another instance, David says, "Indignation grips me because of the wicked, who have forsaken your law"(v. 53). Later he says, "I look on the faithless with loathing, for they do not *obey* your word"(v. 158).

Just as the godly man fulfills his duty to *obey* the Lord's commands, the ungodly man rejects that duty. He is like Jeroboam, king of Israel, whom God confronts through the prophet Ahijah saying: "I tore the kingdom away from the house of David and gave it to you, but you have not been like my servant David, who kept my commands and followed me with all his heart, doing only what was right in my eyes. You have done more evil than all those before you"(1 Kings 14:8-9).

The duty to *obey* God's commands and avoid Jeroboam's folly is further highlighted by the lives of God's priests, the Levites. Their scrupulous care of God's dwelling place and ritual sacrifices perhaps best demonstrates their obedience. Speaking of the tribe of Levi, the Lord says, "They are to perform duties for him [Aaron] and for the whole community at the Tent of Meeting by doing the work of the tabernacle"(Num 3:7). Nehemiah further reminds us that these duties were often individualized (Neh 13:30). But contrary to what some might think, these specific "duties of the Tent" were not given to the Levites as onerous work (Num 18:3). They were not some kind of punishment or penance. Rather, God meant them as a gift: "I am giving you the service of the priesthood as a gift"(18:7). When was the last time we considered our duties to serve God as a "gift"?

Regardless of its perception as a gift or a burden, duty's specific responsibilities further extended from the Temple and the palace into the more intimate filial and familial realms of every Israelite. One of the recurring themes of the Old Testament is the duty to care for the widowed wife. Under Old Testament law, the brother of a deceased man had the familial and conjugal duty to assume responsibility for his brother's widowed wife. Perhaps the most memorable story involving this duty arises in Christ's familial line. It is the somewhat troubling account of Tamar (Gen 38).

Tamar was the widow of Er, son of Judah. When Er died, his brother, Onan, was told to assume his duty as a brother-in-law. This duty included sleeping with Tamar and producing offspring in the name of Er. In his wickedness, however, Onan shirked his conjugal duty by spilling his semen on the ground to prevent the production of offspring that would not be his. As a result of this wickedness, God put Onan to death. Subsequently, Tamar remained without child.

Ultimately, in her desperation for an offspring, Tamar posed as a prostitute when Er's father, Judah, came into town. In her ruse, Judah was beguiled into sleeping with her. The result: twins, Perez and Zerah. The former is in the line of Christ.

In perhaps a more redeeming and encouraging view of familial duty, the Old Testament gives us the story of Boaz. Unlike Onan, Boaz was a man of godly character. Into his life, God brings Ruth, the daughter-in-law of Naomi and the widow of Kilion. After the death of her husband, Ruth left her homeland of Moab and followed Naomi to Bethlehem. In this new place, without a husband, she was dependent on the land for her livelihood. Therefore, one day she goes out to the fields to gather the leftover grain. She is noticed by the landowner Boaz. In his kindness, he offers her the protection and provision of his property.

When Naomi finds out where Ruth has gleaned the grain, she is delighted. Boaz is one of Ruth's kinsman-redeemers (a relative who has the responsibility to care for a relation in trouble). Although there is a nearer kinsman, he is not interested in assuming his duty to Ruth. He says to Boaz, "I might endanger my own estate....I cannot do it"(Ruth 4:6). As a man of honor, however, Boaz says, "if he is not willing, as surely as the Lord lives I will do it"(Ruth 3:13). Boaz then proceeds to marry Ruth and do his familial duty to Ruth and the Lord.

The offspring of this union is Obed. Like Tamar's son Perez, Obed is also in the lineage of the future King David and, ultimately, Christ Himself. The inclusion of these two disparate stories within His family tree is no mistake. The juxtaposed disobedience of Onan and the contrasting obedience of Boaz demonstrates for us the importance God places on our duty to Him.

The story of Ruth also reminds us that biblical women often best demonstrated the coupling of familial duty with the servant's call to dutiful obedience.

Ruth faithfully *obeys* her mother-in-law Naomi and simultaneously describes herself as a "servant" before Boaz. Hannah, the mother of the prophet Samuel, Abigail the wife of David, and even Mary, the mother of Jesus, were all dutiful wives and mothers who also describe themselves as "servants" ready to *obey*. Mary, in particular, embodies a remarkably dutiful obedience. When told she will bear the Son of God, she simply says, "'I am the Lord's servant...May it be to me as you have said'"(Luke 1:38).

But while Mary's obedience is exemplary, her greatest contribution to our understanding of dutiful obedience rests in the fruit of her womb: Jesus Christ. Jesus serves as the paragon of an obedience rooted in the duty of a servant. The Lord says of Him, "'Here is my chosen servant, whom I uphold, my chosen one in whom I delight"(Is 42:1). The Apostle Paul goes on to describe Christ's amazing role as "servant." He says, Jesus, "Who being in very nature God, did not consider equality with God something to be grasped, but made himself nothing, taking the very nature of a servant..." (Phil 2:6-7). Though Jesus was rightfully "Master" (Luke 8:24, 9:49, 9:33), He made Himself a servant. And as a servant, He repeatedly chose to accept His duty to *obey* the Father.

Sometimes this commitment to *obey* the Lord even required Jesus to *obey* other human beings. As a child, he dutifully obeyed His parents. We are told, "Then He went down to Nazareth with [His parents] and was obedient to them"(Luke 2:51). In this spirit of obedience, Jesus says, "For even the Son of Man did not come to be served, but to serve..."(Mark 10:45). So when Jesus then says, "'A student is not above his teacher, nor a servant above his master," we can be confident that He expects us to also accept our duty to *obey* (Matt 10:24).

As He so often does in Scripture, Jesus further illustrates this truth in one of His many parables. As the Gospel of Luke recounts, Jesus tells the short parable of the servant coming in from the fields. Putting the disciples in the theoretical position of "master," Jesus asks: "Would he [the master] say to the servant when he comes in from the field, 'Come along now and sit down to eat?' Would he not rather say, 'Prepare my supper, get yourself ready and wait on me while I eat and drink; after that you may eat and drink'?" Going further, Jesus asks: "Would he thank the servant because he did what he was told to do? So you also, when you have done everything you were told to do, should say, 'We are unworthy servants; we have only done our duty'"(Luke 17:7-10).

Perhaps too often, we see duty in our lives more like the rebellious Onan than the unworthy servant that Christ calls us to emulate. But as Jesus clearly tells us, duty involves expected responsibility. No life escapes it —not even Christ's. Jesus' prayer in the Garden of Gethsemane reminds us that even He had to choose to embrace a duty He might not have initially desired (Matt 26:39-42).

And yet, Jesus and the godly men and women of Scripture demonstrate that this dutiful obedience is not ultimately a burden, but a source of praise. While we are free to meet our duties to the Lord with churlish disobedience or grudging acquiescence, we are encouraged to embrace them with a joyful and willing spirit that says, "I delight in your decrees; I will not neglect your Word"(Ps 119:16). Like Christ, we are called to see our duty to God's will as the "food" of our souls: "'My food,' said Jesus, 'is to do the will of Him who sent me and to finish His work'"(John 4:34).

In light of these examples, it is worth pausing to ask ourselves: How are we responding to our duties to Christ and His people? Do we see them and the obedience they require of us as gifts from God? Are they the food of our spirits? Are we daily meeting our duty to *obey* God's commands with a spirit more like Onan and Jeroboam or Boaz and David?

Regardless of the attitude we bring to obedience, the fact remains: We have a duty to *obey* the Lord. Indeed, as Soren Kierkegaard reminds us, we have an "absolute duty to God" which must serve to inspire our obedience. At every opportunity to *obey*, we must seek to act "as though there were a superior measure of moral performance that made social intentions irrelevant; …an absolute duty to God that overrides the ethical…," and motivates us to do all that Christ requires of us.[37] When we embrace this absolute duty, then God enables us to *obey*: "In Christ and the Holy Spirit He [God] has made most wonderful provision for fulfilling His engagement."[38]

In light of this hope, the Christian who is filled with the Spirit does not resist the responsibilities of duty. He delights in them! He sees his role as servant, even a slave of righteousness, as a precious gift of God and a glorious opportunity to emulate the obedience of Christ Himself (Rom 6:15-23). He rejoices in the occasion to "discharge all the duties of [his] ministry"(2 Tim 4:5) in the service of Jesus. He sees duty as an essential instrument in the *joy of obeying* the God he loves. And ultimately, his Spirit-filled life strives to say, like Paul before his accusers, "I have fulfilled my duty to God in all good conscience to this day"(Acts 23:1).

---

[37] Soren Kierkegaard, *Fear and Trembling* (London: Penguin Books, 2003), 108, 28.

[38] Andrew Murray, *The School of Obedience* (Public Domain).

6.

The Great "Because…"

For God is the King of all the earth….
—*Psalm 47:7*

But because you [Jesus] say so, I will….
—*Luke 5:5*

Our daily duties often remind us: Every act of obedience requires submission. Whether powered by the duress of force or the willing pleasure of love, to *obey* we must submit ourselves to someone or something. This reality may cause the child to ask his parents, or the Christian to ask God, "Why? Why must I *obey*?" Parents and God alike may simply respond: "*Because* I said so."

But unless we are convinced this "*Because…*" holds our best interest, or we are compelled by the force of love or persuaded by a power we cannot deny, it may still be extremely difficult for us to *obey*. Our submission requires an admittance and acceptance of a power differential. Very few of us like to acknowledge a position of weakness or inferiority. And while this discrepancy in authority might be limited to the individual act of obedience, it may also extend to the continuing and fixed parameters of the relationship: Parent-child, boss-employee, government-citizen. In any scenario, however, to *obey* we must willingly submit or, at least, acquiesce.

No where is the power differential of obedience, and the submission required in it, more pronounced than in the relationship between God and man. In the days of monarchies, the world had a much clearer understanding of unconditional obedience to an unrivaled power. When the king spoke, the subject obeyed. Failure to do so often meant death, torture, imprisonment, or estrangement. Didn't King Solomon say, "A king's wrath strikes terror like the roar of a lion; those who anger him forfeit their lives"(Prov 20:2)? Within these clear lines of power, obedience to a Divine King may have been more comprehensible.

But in today's more egalitarian age, obeying out of respect for a divinely appointed authority (or God Himself) is largely an anachronism. Yet are we to believe the divine power paradigm monarchies imperfectly embodied no longer matters simply because monarchal authority has all but vanished? Or, does God, the Everlasting and Omnipotent King, deserve our obedience—*just because*?

God Himself uses this simple justification for obedience in the middle of His Levitical Law. He says to the people of Israel, "You are to be holy to me *because* I, the Lord, am holy, and I have set you apart from the nations to be my own"(Lev 20:26). The Israelites were commanded to be holy before God *because* God Himself is holy. Ultimately, all obedience to God can be justified simply *because* of who God is: "'I AM WHO I AM'"(Ex 3:14).

The role of King is one of the "Great I AM's" most prominent roles in both Scripture and our lives. The Word of God repeatedly reminds us of His royalty, majesty, and power. As a king himself, David might have understood "kingly" attributes (and the obedience they inspire) better than most. Near the end of his life, David stood before the assembly of Israel and declared God's royal majesty. He says:

> Praise be to you, O Lord, God of our father Israel, from everlasting to everlasting. Yours, O Lord, is the greatness and the power and the glory and the majesty and the splendor, for everything in heaven and earth is yours. Yours, O Lord, is the kingdom, you are exalted as head over all. Wealth and honor come from you; you are the ruler of all things. In your hands are strength and power to exalt and give strength to all. Now, our God, we give you thanks and praise your glorious name (1 Chron 29: 10-13).

In the Psalms, David goes on to reinforce these attributes and further link them to God's title of King. He says, "Who is this King of glory? The Lord strong and mighty, the Lord mighty in battle"(Ps 24:8). In another place he says, "The Lord is enthroned as King forever"(Ps 29:10). David even proceeds to declare God's kingship over all other gods: "For the Lord is the great God, the great King of all gods"(Ps 95:3).

This royal designation is reiterated by other Psalmists as well. The Sons of Korah exclaim, "You are my King and my God..."(Ps 44:4). In another place they sing, "How awesome is the Lord Most High, the great King over all the earth"(Ps 47:2). Asaph says, "But you, O God, are my King from of old; you bring salvation upon the earth"(Ps 74:12).

The Apostle Paul echoes this spirit of the Psalms in the New Testament. In his letter to Timothy, Paul describes the Lord as, "God, the blessed and only Ruler, the King of kings and Lord of lords, who alone is immortal and who lives in unapproachable light, whom no one has seen or can see. To Him be honor and might forever"(1 Tim 6:15-16).

In declaring God King, Paul and the Psalmists before him define their place beneath the almighty and omnipotent power of God. David speaks even further from this diminutive position in Psalm 145. He says, "I will exalt you, my God the King; I will praise your name forever and ever....Great is the Lord and most worthy of praise; His greatness no one can fathom"(Ps 145: 1, 3). To exalt another as David does, we must recognize their superiority. We must be willing to bow down.

As a king himself, David shows us the importance of this spiritual diminution before God. He understands genuflection of the heart as an act of worship made possible by obedience. And in saying "Be exalted, O God, above the heavens, let your glory be over all the earth"(Ps 57:11), David shows us how to appreciate God's "kingship" as "central in the life of God in the soul."[39]

But how far our contemporary world has wandered from this truth! Current culture suggests that we must be kings and queens of our own lives, obedient to nothing but self-interest. David and the other Psalmists could not disagree more. Indeed, the Psalmists emphasize the exact opposite: We are honored and blessed when God is the Great King in our lives. To this point, A.W. Tozer flips contemporary dogma upside down when he says:

> Let no one imagine that he will lose anything of human dignity by this voluntary sell-out of his all to his God. He does not by this degrade himself as a man; rather he finds his right place of high honor as one made in the image of his Creator. His deep disgrace lay in his moral derangement, his unnatural usurpation of the place of God. His honor will be proved by

---

[39] A.W. Tozer, *The Pursuit of God* in *The Classic Works of A.W. Tozer* (Public Domain), 60.

> restoring again that stolen throne. In exalting God over all he finds his own highest honor upheld.[40]

As Tozer points out, our best is bound up in our willingness to see God as the King of our lives. And our humble obedience before Him best testifies to this worshipful inclination of the heart. Therefore, we are at our most spiritually healthy when we have the capacity to say with King David, "But who am I...," and "O Lord, what is man that you care for him, the son of man that you think of him?"(1 Chron 29:14; Ps 144:3).

In exalting God and claiming Him as King of our lives, we further recognize His absolute sovereignty. As King, God's control reaches into every "realm" of His Kingdom. David says, "The Lord has established His throne in heaven, and His kingdom rules over all"(Ps 103:19). And while the world might encourage us to resist the power and authority He wields from that throne, Scripture encourages us to welcome and rejoice in it. Again, King David serves as an exemplar in this election.

In perhaps one of the most focused descriptions of God's kingly sovereignty, Psalm 145 goes from an initial exaltation of "God the King" to a catalogue of His power, splendor, and majesty. David says God's people will "commend [His] works to another; they will tell of [His] mighty acts. They will speak of the glorious splendor of [His] majesty..."(v. 4-5). The generations will "tell of the power of [His] awesome works, and...proclaim [His] great deeds"(v. 6). Continuing, he says, "They will tell of the glory of [His] kingdom and speak of [His] might, so that all men may

---

[40] 61

know of [His] mighty acts and the glorious splendor of [His] kingdom"(v. 11-12). For, God's "kingdom is an everlasting kingdom, and [His] dominion endures through all generations"(v. 13). The kingly majesty David describes in these verses should enthuse an awe-inspired obedience in the hearts of His people.

But where the motive force of the King's majesty and splendor might fail to inspire our obedience, His royal benevolence may move our hardened hearts to *obey*. David describes the "abundant goodness" of a King whose sovereignty in our lives is "gracious and compassionate, slow to anger and rich in love"(v. 7-8). He goes on to say that the King is "good to all" and "faithful to all His promises and loving toward all He has made"(v. 9, 13). God the King "upholds all those who fall and lifts up all who are bowed down"(v. 14). The King even opens His hand to "satisfy the desires of every living thing"(v. 16). This King is anything but a tyrannical autocrat. His kingly "goodness," therefore, ought to energize our obedience.

Yet, if we find our hearts calloused and disobedient even in the face of the King's majesty and goodness, let us remember He is also a King of justice. The Psalmist says, "Righteousness and justice are the foundation of [His] throne"(Ps 89:14). In another place, the Sons of Korah say, "Your throne, O God, will last for ever and ever; a scepter of justice will be the scepter of your kingdom"(Ps 45: 6). David follows by saying, "The Lord reigns forever; He has established His throne for judgment. He will judge the world in righteousness; He will govern the peoples with justice"(Ps 9:7-8).

The prophet Isaiah reiterates the Psalms: "For the Lord is a God of justice"(Is 30:18). This knowledge then causes Isaiah to cry out, "'Woe is me!'…'I am ruined! For I am a man of unclean lips, and I live among a people of unclean lips, and my eyes have seen the King, the Lord Almighty'"(Is 6:5). Have we, like the Psalmists and Isaiah, considered "God the King" as our Royal Judge? Have we failed to remember His judgement will one day destine some for eternal life and others for the lake of fire (Rev 20:12, 15)? Where splendor and goodness fail to stimulate our obedience, surely the King's justice must prevail upon us to *obey*!

Ultimately, any consideration of biblical justice must also include the person of Jesus Christ. In addition to being the Son of God and our Savior, Jesus is also Judge and King. Peter describes Christ as the "Judge of the living and the dead"(Acts 10:42). Jesus Himself says, "Moreover, the Father judges no one, but has entrusted all judgement to the Son…"(John 5:22). This role of "Judge" goes hand in hand with His kingship.

From beginning to end, the New Testament is bookended with images reminding us of Christ's kingship. His narrative begins with the visiting Magi who recognize and honor Jesus' royalty. They travel hundreds of miles to bow down and worship Jesus, bringing Him gifts fit for a king (Matt 2:11). Even King Herod recognizes Jesus as a kingly threat. He murders all the male children in Bethlehem under the age of two to prevent the prophesied King from usurping his throne (Matt 2:16). Herod takes Jesus' kingship so seriously it cost many lives.

But Jesus the King escapes Herod. And, in Christ's triumphal resurrection, even death itself. The New Testament then ends with images of Christ returning as the Conquering King of the world. He leads the armies of heaven, "dressed in a robe dipped with blood"(Rev 19:13-14). The Apostle John says, "Out of His mouth comes a sharp sword with which to strike down the nations. 'He will rule them with an iron scepter.' He treads the winepress of the fury of the wrath of God Almighty"(Rev 19:15). And, on His robe will be written, "KING OF KINGS AND LORD OF LORDS"(Rev 19:16).

This Conquering King shall judge us all. As the Apostle Paul reminds us, "For we must all appear before the judgement seat of Christ, that each may receive what is due him for the things done while in the body, whether good or bad"(2 Cor 5:10). In the reality of this coming day, we are wise to *obey*. Christ our Judge has enjoined us to this effort (John 14:15).

However, in our efforts to *obey*, let us never despair. Let us trust in the grace of the King who saves us and is "able to keep you from falling and present you before His glorious presence without fault…"(Jude 1:24). In Christ our King, we, like Paul before us, can hope for the "crown of righteousness, which the Lord, the righteous Judge, will award to…all who have longed for His appearing"(2 Tim 4:8). To this King, "be glory, majesty, power and authority, through Jesus Christ our Lord, before all ages, now and forevermore!"(Jude 1:25). To this King, may we commit to joyfully *obey—just because*!

7.

The Wind and the Waves

You answer us with awesome deeds of righteousness,
O God our Savior...
who stilled the roaring of the seas,
the roaring of their waves....
—Psalm 65:5,7

"Even the wind and the waves obey Him!"
—Matthew 8:27

The crashing surf and the spiraling hurricane winds attest to this truth: Nature is filled with incredible power. It can level cities, pick up buildings, and swallow ships. Its strength demands respect and inspires obedience in animals and humans alike.

But from where does that strength—and the obedience it requires—emanate if not from the Creator Himself? As Oswald Chambers says, "When a man comes face to face with Nature, God seems to be almighty against all his conceptions."[41] And like His roles as King and Judge, God's role as Creator further draws our hearts to a worshipful obedience. For this reason, to fully understand and appreciate obedience and the ensuing joy we are to find in it, we must also recognize God as our Creator. We must see Him standing over and within His glorious creation.

---

[41] Oswald Chambers, *Baffled to Fight Better* in *The Complete Works of Oswald Chambers* (Grand Rapids: Discover House Publishers, 2000), 57-58.

With this perspective, Genesis commences with God (*Elohim*) as Creator: "In the beginning God created the heavens and the earth"(Gen 1:1). In subsequent verses we see God the Creator forming light and darkness, the fish of the sea, the birds of the air, and man and woman, made in His own image (Gen 1:2-27). Considering this creative genius and power, the prophet Jeremiah says, "God made the earth by His power; He founded the world by His wisdom and stretched out the heavens by His understanding"(Jer 10:12). This knowledge causes King David to further exclaim, "How many are your works, O Lord! In wisdom you made them all; the earth is full of your creatures"(Ps 104:24).

As David suggests, the sheer multiplicity, much less the biologic complexity and beauty of God's creatures and the universe they inhabit, remind us of who God is: Creator. He is the Potter who looks to His creation and says, "I, the Lord, have created it"(Is 45:8). And as a result, His divine qualities permeate everything we see: "For since the creation of the world God's invisible qualities—His eternal power and divine nature—have been clearly seen, being understood from what has been made, so that we are without excuse"(Rom 1:20).

Creation, as the Apostle Paul opines, continually directs us away from the indefensible position of ignorance of God's almighty power towards an undeniable knowledge of our Almighty Creator. In its natural majesty, creation demonstrates His divine qualities and glorifies His name. It reminds us that we too are created beings. And ultimately, in this parity, creation teaches us the importance of obedience and how we are to *obey*.

To initiate our exploration of the obedience demonstrated in creation, we must remember the fundamental paradigm of obeying: It implies a submission to or dependence upon a superior power. While we might readily understand obedience as it relates to a master, king, or judge, nature has no conception of these social positions. But, creation and its creatures are vitally familiar with biologic dependence and hierarchy; and, as a result, a perhaps unconscious, yet undeniable obedience to the Creator and His will. In this way, creation's first lesson for us in obedience is the recognition and declaration of God as Creator.

This truth became painfully (quite literally) obvious to Job amidst his own physical suffering. Looking to creation, he says to his friends: "'But ask the animals, and they will teach you; or the birds of the air, and they will tell you; or speak to the earth, and it will teach you, or let the fish of the sea inform you. Which of all these does not know that the hand of the Lord has done this? In His hand is the life of every creature and the breath of all mankind'"(Job 12:7-10). Job recognizes in creation a declaration of God as Creator.

Further articulating this declaration, David says, "The heavens declare the glory of God; the skies proclaim the work of His hands. Day after day they pour forth speech; night after night they display knowledge"(Ps 19:1-2). In the world around him, David sees evidence of God's creative power: He "makes the clouds His chariot"; "makes springs pour water into the ravines"; "waters the mountains from His upper chambers"; and "makes grass grow for the cattle"(Ps 104: 3, 10, 13, 14). Observing these feats, David sees God as "the Maker of heaven and earth, the sea, and everything in them—the Lord, who remains faithful forever"(Ps 146:6). Creation further inspires David to say, "Great are the works of the Lord; they are pondered by all who delight in them"(Ps 111:2).

This contemplation of God as Creator then causes David to consider his own position in creation. He recognizes that he too is a creature created by God. David says, "Know that the Lord is God. It is He who has made us, and we are His; we are His people, the sheep of His pasture"(Ps 100:3). In another place He says, "He is our God and we are the people of His pasture, the flock under His care"(Ps 95:7). Few creatures are more dependent than sheep. And yet, as David contemplates God as Creator and his own place in creation, he compares himself to these feeble animals.

In this spirit of humble introspection, David continues by exclaiming, "When I consider your heavens, the work of your fingers, the moon and the stars, which you have set in place, what is man that you are mindful of him, the son of man that you care for him?"(Ps 8:3-4). This wonderment grows as David then ponders God's hand in his own creation. He says, "For you created my inmost being; you knit me together in my mother's womb"(Ps 139:13). Going on David says, "My frame was not hidden from you when I was made in the secret place. When I was woven together in the depths of the earth, your eyes saw my unformed body"(v. 15-16). This intimate knowledge ultimately causes David to rejoice. He says, "I praise you because I am fearfully and wonderfully made; your works are wonderful, I know that full well"(v. 14).

Other godly men in Scripture also evidence their contemplation of God as Creator and Sustainer of their physical forms. One of the recurring motifs used to express these divine roles invokes the potter and his clay. The prophet Isaiah says, "We are the clay, you are the Potter; we are all the work of your hand"(Is 64:8). In another place, this thought then causes Isaiah to consider his dependent and vulnerable position. The prophet says, "Does the clay say to the potter, 'What are you making?'"(Is 45:9).

Jeremiah contemplates similarly. After going down to a potter's house and observing the creation of a pot, he notes the potter "shaping it [the pot] as seemed best to him"(Jer 18:4). God, the Potter, then speaks to Jeremiah: "'Like clay in the hand of the potter, so are you in my hand, O house of Israel'"(v. 6).

Even the Apostle Paul alludes to this Creator motif in his letter to the Romans. He says, "Shall what is formed say to him who formed it, 'Why did you make me like this?' Does not the potter have the right to make out of the same lump of clay some pottery for noble purposes and some for common use?"(Rom 9:20-21). And if so, why do we as "jars of clay"(2 Cor 4:7) so often forget our place in the hands of the Maker?

Creation, however, never forgets God is the Creator and Sustainer of all things. This knowledge demonstrates itself in creation's *absolute obedience*. The Apostles saw this firsthand on the tumultuous waters of the Sea of Galilee. When Christ rebukes the wind and the waves saying, "'Quiet! Be Still!,'" the disciples witness an immediate calming of the storm. They exclaim: "'Who is this? Even the wind and the waves *obey* Him!'"(Mark 4:39, 41). In their incredulity, however, they had forgotten the Psalmist's words: "stormy winds...do His bidding"(Ps 148:8). In their amazement, they failed to remember Jeremiah's rebuke of Israel: "When He [God] thunders, the waters in the heavens roar; He makes clouds rise from the ends of the earth. He sends lightning with the rain and brings out the wind from His storehouses"(Jer 10:12-13).

This obedience of the wind and the waters embodies creation's ongoing testimony of "the image of the invisible God, the firstborn of all creation"(Col

1:15). When the winds abate and the waves become still before Christ, nature testifies to Him through whom "all things were created: things in heaven and on earth, visible and invisible, whether thrones or powers or rulers or authorities; all things were created by Him and for Him. He is before all things, and in Him all things hold together"(Col 1:16-17). In every strand of DNA and connective tissue, every nebula and galaxy scattered across the universe, creation declares: Christ is the "Alpha and the Omega, the First and the Last, the Beginning and the End"(Rev 22:13). He is the "ruler of God's creation"(Rev 3:14), the Creator and Sustainer of all things.

Reminded by creation of God's role as Creator, we are then called to observe how nature's obedience may further inform our own obedience. David again serves as our example in this lesson. Witnessing the heaven's declaration of the "glory of God," he notes how the sun is "like a champion rejoicing to run his course"(Ps 19: 1, 5). David observes joyful obedience from even that celestial "power" from whom no one can hide (v. 6). This demonstration of obedience then leads David to consider God's commands for his own life. He says, "The law of the Lord is perfect," and "The precepts of the Lord are right, giving joy to the heart. The commands of the Lord are radiant, giving light to the eyes"(v. 7-8). He concludes this consideration saying, "By them [God's commands] is your servant warned; in keeping them there is great reward"(v. 11).

David's example demonstrates for us how the heavens and the sun, as well as all the rest of God's creatures, instruct us in obedience. As Soren Kierkegaard similarly notes, they are "the obedient teachers"[42] in *unconditional obedience.* This is creation's second lesson in the *joy of obeying.* Whether it is in the wind, the waves, the rustling leaves or the singing birds, Kierkegaard notes "every sound, every sound you hear, it is all compliance, unconditional obedience, so that in it you can hear God as you can hear Him in the music of the obedient movement of the heavenly bodies."[43]

Looking specifically to the biblical example of the lily of the field and the bird of the air, Kierkegaard notes their position of dependence; and, in this position of vulnerability, their ensuing acceptance of, and obedience to, God's unconditional will.[44] Brilliantly, Kierkegaard goes on to note that man alone in creation appears to believe that conditional obedience is acceptable—perhaps even preferable. The lily and the bird know nothing of this. Indeed, he says, "That the least bit of disobedience would truly have any name other than contempt for God is something that the lily and the bird cannot and do not want to understand."[45]

This "contempt" for God appears not only in our own lives, but also in countless Old Testament examples. From the original sin in the Garden of Eden, to Israel's repeated flirtations with idolatry, we see an attempt to justify what Kierkegaard calls "half-measures."[46] We give part of who we are, but not the

---

[42] Soren Kierkegaard, *The Lily of the Field and the Bird of the Air* (Princeton: Princeton University Press, 2016), 46.

[43] 49.

[44] 50.

[45] 50.

[46] 50.

whole. We do lip service to God, then do what we want.

One story that illustrates this tendency appears in the Book of Judges. A man named Micah is given a pile of silver from his mother. With it, he fashions an idol and creates an ephod which he then places in a shrine. He even installs priests—first one of his sons, and then a passing Levite. All of this he purportedly does in the name of the Lord, because in those days, "everyone did as he saw fit"(Judg 17:6).

For a time, Micah convinces himself that this syncretic and mixed, "half-measure" of personalized obedience would earn God's blessing. But eventually, he finds otherwise. An army of Danites comes and steals the idol, the ephod, and even the priest. Micah is left with nothing. And, "seeing that they [the Danites] were too strong for him, [Micah] turned around and went home"(Judg 18:26). In his disobedience to God, Micah loses everything.

Micah's example serves as a foil for the lily of the field. Micah believed he knew best. Rather than dependence, he strove for autonomous independence. He did as "he saw fit." But ironically, in his efforts for freedom, he found the shackles of destitution.

The lily, however, teaches us that *absolute dependence*, and *unconditional obedience*, is freedom. As Jesus says, "See how the lilies of the field grow. They do not labor or spin. Yet I tell you that not even Solomon in all of his splendor was dressed like one of these. If that is how God clothes the grass of the field, which is here today and tomorrow is thrown into the fire, will He not much more clothe you, O you of little faith?"(Matt 6:28-30). The lily has no cares because it is absolutely dependent upon its Creator.

In this position of dependence and *unconditional obedience*, the lily teaches us how to become exactly what we are intended to be. As Kierkegaard further notes, because the lily "was unconditionally obedient...it became itself in loveliness; it actually became its entire possibility...."[47] Whereas Micah did what he thought was best and found nothing, the lily obediently surrenders to God's will and finds total fulfillment. It decides to "bloom where it is planted." In so doing, the lily, like the bird of the air and all the rest of creation, teaches us how, in the words of Thomas Merton, "to fulfill our destiny, according to God's will, to be what God wants us to be."[48] Our unconditional obedience to God's will leads us to our spiritual fruition.

This realization of fulfillment is reason enough to find joy in obeying. Our contemporary world flounders in efforts at self-exploration, definition, and actualization simply because it has failed to learn from creation how unconditional obedience leads to our consummation in God. But let us not be fooled: creation stands witness to our willful disobedience. As Moses told the Israelites, "This day I call heaven and earth as witnesses against you that I have set before you life and death....Now choose life...that you may love the Lord your God, listen to His voice, and hold fast to Him"(Deut 30:19-20). Therefore, under the watchful eyes of an earth that bows down before the Creator (Ps 66:4), let us choose life! Let us, like the lilies of the fields and the birds of the air, rejoice in who God has designed us to be: creatures filled with the *joy of obeying*.

---

[47] Soren Kierkegaard, *The Lily of the Field and the Bird of the Air* (Princeton: Princeton University Press, 2016), 55.

[48] Thomas Merton, *No Man is an Island* (New York: Harcourt, 1983), 131.

8.

Agape: The Beloved's Love

But God, being rich in mercy, because of the great love with which He loved us...made us alive together with Christ....
—*Ephesians 2:4-5*

I love you, O Lord, my strength.
—*Psalm 18:1*

The beauty and majesty of creation constantly remind us of God's love. In the colors of the rainbow and a baby's smile, God declares: "You are my Beloved!" Indeed, love is the golden thread woven throughout God's story. From start to finish, it traces through and wraps around His redemptive narrative for the human race. It is the gift we do not deserve and yet receive, nonetheless. It is the warm embrace of a Father for His beloved children. It is, as the poet Rilke says, "the song we sing in every silence."[49] God's story is a love story.

    Within this narrative frame, it should then come as little surprise that the ultimate motive force behind the *joy of obeying* is: Love. The Apostle John speaks to this power when he says, "This is love: not that we loved God, but that He loved us and sent His Son as an atoning sacrifice for our sins"(1 John 4:10). Going on, he says, "We love because He first loved us," and "Everyone who loves has been born of God and knows God"(v. 19, 7). Ultimately, "God is love. Whoever lives in love lives in God, and God in Him"(v. 16).

---

[49] Rainer Rilke, *Rilke's Book of Hours: Love Poems to God* (New York: Riverhead Books, 2005), 89.

Because God's presence is synonymous with love, Christians must, therefore, exude it. When His Spirit is alive and well within us, our lives naturally overflow with His love. And, while the Apostle John rightly reminds us that this overflow will demonstrate itself in our love for others (1 John 4:11, 21), he carefully posits that this love must be preceded by a love for God Himself. He says, "This is how we know that we love the children of God: by loving God and carrying out His commands. This is love for God: to *obey* His commands"(1 John 5:2-3).

In these words, John strikes to the heart of the matter: Love for God (and by extension, for His children) necessitates obedience. Jesus said this very thing to John and the other Apostles: "If you love me, you will *obey* what I command"(John 14:15). For emphasis He repeated it: "If anyone loves me, he will *obey* my teaching. My Father will love him, and we will come to him and make our home with him. He who does not love me will not *obey* my teaching"(v. 23-24). Clearly, if we say we love Christ, we must *obey*!

Love is, therefore, forgetting all other arguments, the primary reason to *obey* the Lord. And because any love that is true is Love Himself, it knows joy in the process of obeying. For when we love, God's Spirit in us loves God Himself, for otherwise a "house divided against itself will not stand"(Matt 12:25). Indeed, God's Spirit is "jealous" in His love for the glory of His name amongst His people (Ex 20:5). As the prophet Ezekiel records: "'This is what the Sovereign Lord says: It is not for your sake, O house of Israel, that I am going to do these things, but for the sake of my holy name....I will show the holiness of my great name....Then the nations will know that I am the Lord...when I show myself holy through you before their eyes'"(Ezek 36:22-24).

Yet despite God's passion for His name, let us not for a moment think obedience will be easy simply because it involves God's Spirit loving God Himself. Such thinking demonstrates we do not understand love. For love is hard work, or it is not love. God Himself is no exception. May we merely pause to consider the agonizing cost of God's love for us in the sacrifice of Christ (1 John 4:10)!

This gift of Calvary also demonstrates God's love is greater than anyone can ever know (Eph 3:19-21). And in the force of this Almighty love, the Spirit's empowerment then ensures obedience is not beyond our capabilities. As Thomas Merton notes, "He [the Spirit] not only makes us understand…God's love as it is manifested to us in Christ, but He also makes us live by that love and experience its action in our hearts."[50] With the Spirit's motive force, we can then embrace the truth of John's words: "His [God's] commands are not burdensome, for everyone born of God overcomes the world"(1 John 5:3-4). This reiterates what Moses said to the Israelites:

> Now what I am commanding you today is not too difficult for you or beyond your reach. It is not up in heaven, so that you have to ask, 'Who will ascend into heaven to get it and proclaim it to us so we may *obey* it?' Nor is it beyond the sea, so that you have to ask, 'Who will cross the sea to get it and proclaim it to us so we may *obey* it?' No, the word is very near you; it is in your mouth and in your heart so you may *obey* it (Deut 30:11-14).

---

[50]Thomas Merton, *No Man is an Island* (New York: Harcourt, 1983), 176.

As Christ is the Word who became flesh and now resides in us, we have hope: We are born of God, we have overcome the world, and we have within us the power of Love to *obey* His commands (John 1:1, 14; Rom 8:10). In this hope there is reason to rejoice in our obeying!

We can find further joy in obeying when we consider some of the specific scriptural manifestations of the love of God within us. One of the most important of these themes involves God's role as Father. Indeed, arguably, we cannot understand the character and depth of scriptural love without appreciating God as "*Abba*! Father!"(Roman 8:15).

Emphasizing this truth, the Apostle John exclaims, "How great is the love the Father has lavished on us, that we should be called children of God!"(1 John 3:1). In this declaration, John voices centuries of Jewish tradition recognizing God as Father. From the writings of Moses, through the Prophets, and straight down to Jesus Christ and His Apostles, all of them declare God as Father.

Beginning this conversation, Moses says to the people of Israel, "Is He [God] not your Father, your Creator, who made you and formed you?"(Deut 32:6). The prophet Isaiah later declares before God, "But you are our Father, though Abraham does not know us or Israel acknowledge us; you, O Lord, are our Father, our Redeemer from of old is your name"(Is 63:16). And the prophet Malachi closes the Old Testament by rhetorically asking, "Have we not all one Father?"(Mal 2:10).

With this Old Testament understanding of God as Father, Jesus Christ then enters the world as the Son of God. The Father says of Him, "'This is my Son, whom I love; with Him I am well pleased'"(Matt 3:17). Through the obedience of the Son, God's love then manifests itself among us in all of its spectacular glory. As Jesus reminds us: "For God so loved the world that He gave His one and only Son, that whoever believes in Him shall not perish but have eternal life"(John 3:16).

In this ultimate gift of a Father's love, we see the divine completion of Abraham's sacrifice of Isaac (Gen 22). Prefiguring Christ's work, Abraham offered up Isaac to God in a trusting and loving obedience. But because of God's fatherly love, He spared Isaac, just as He spares us. A ram was provided for Abraham's sacrifice. A Lamb, Christ our Lord, was provided for us.

But unlike the symbolic ram caught in the thicket before Abraham, Christ was not a victim of His Father's sacrificial love. In His unity with the Father, Jesus was the knowing and willing vehicle of God's redeeming gift to the world (John 10:30). He chose to obey because "the world must learn that I [Jesus] love the Father and that I do exactly what my Father has commanded me"(John 14:31). Christ's love powered His volitional obedience to lay down His life: "No one takes it [my life] from me, but I lay it down of my own accord. I have the authority to lay it down and authority to take it up again"(John 10:18). In this ultimate sacrifice, Jesus demonstrated for us how obedience fulfills what He called the greatest act of love: "Greater love has no man than this, that he lay down his life for his friends"(John 15:13). And, as Christ reminds us, we are His friends (v. 15)!

With the receipt of this amazing gift of love, however, comes both a privilege and a challenge. Jesus says, "As the Father has loved me, so have I loved you. Now remain in my love. If you *obey* my commands, you will remain in my love, just as I have obeyed my Father's commands and remain in His love"(John 15:9-10). Christ calls us to the privilege of abiding in His love—

and by extension, the Father's love. And then using Himself as the example, He then challenges us to remain in this love through obedience. *Jesus calls us to the obedience of love through the love of obedience.*

This loving desire to *obey* naturally follows from a love of the Father. When we love our *Abba*, the will to *obey* comes as organically and rhythmically as breathing. Nothing delights us more! At the same time, any disobedience ought to bring us to tears before our Father. And yet, we need little reminding: All too often, the sin within us consistently presents an impasse to our joy in obeying.

Knowing this reality, God's Scripture gives us still more encouragement to embrace the love of obedience. One such way includes the Bible's repeated presentations of God's love as the love of a husband for his wife. Speaking through the prophet Isaiah, the Lord says, "For your Maker is your husband—the Lord Almighty is His name"(Is 54:5). In another place he says, "For the Lord will take delight in you, and your land will be married. As a young man marries a maiden, so will your sons marry you; as a bridegroom rejoices over his bride, so will your God rejoice over you"(Is 62:4-5). Invoking the language of a sacred "covenant," Jeremiah similarly says, "I was a husband to them, declares the Lord"(Jer 31:32).

But because of Israel's repeated sin, much of this Old Testament husband and wife metaphor unfortunately includes the language of estrangement or infidelity. Still, while we might hope for a blissfully "happy marriage," this "marital distance" provides the perfect backdrop to display the unrelenting nature of God's love for Israel and for us. As C.S. Lewis notes, in a sense, it is Israel's "woes which are saving the world."⁵¹

Perhaps the finest and most extended example of the marriage metaphor resides in the Book of Hosea. God uses Hosea's marriage to demonstrate His relationship of love with Israel. God says to Hosea, "'Go, take to yourself an adulterous wife and children of unfaithfulness, because the land is guilty of the vilest adultery in departing from the Lord'"(Hosea 1:2). Hosea then *obey*s God and takes the prostitute Gomer as his wife. She conceives and gives birth to children. And yet, as a mirror of the nation of Israel, she falls back into infidelity and reneges on her marriage vows.

But to demonstrate His great forgiveness and His reckless and unrelenting love for His people, God says to Hosea, "'Go, show your love to your wife again, though she is loved by another and is an adulteress. Love her as the Lord loves the Israelites…'"(Hosea 3:1). In obedience, Hosea then reclaims his wife, just as God's love reclaims us.

This language of reconciliatory love echoes in the words of other prophets as well. Isaiah says, "The Lord will call you back as if you were a wife deserted or distressed in spirit—a wife who married young, only to be rejected…but with deep compassion I will bring you back"(Is 54:6-7). In another allegory of infidelity, Ezekiel also describes Israel as an "adulterous wife." After forecasting punishment for her sin, God returns with a promise of reconciliation: "Yet I will remember the covenant I made with you in the days of your youth, and I will establish an everlasting covenant with you"(Ezek 16:60).

---

[51] C.S. Lewis, 'The Grand Miracle,' *God in the Dock* in *The Business of Heaven* (New York: HarperCollins, 1984), 7.

Jesus Christ embodies this everlasting covenant. He is the Bridegroom of heaven (Matt 9:15). And as the Apostle Paul reminds us, we, as God's Church and bride, have been promised to "one husband, to Christ...," that we might be presented to Him as a pure and blameless virgin. In this presentation, we wait for Him as the ten virgins wait on the bridegroom, keeping careful watch by the light of our burning lamps (Matt 25:1-13). While we wait, we ready ourselves in loving obedience. Our hearts fill with joyful anticipation: "Let us rejoice and be glad and give Him glory! For the wedding of the Lamb has come, and His bride has made herself ready!"(Rev 19:7).

Ultimately, in both the Bridegroom and the Father, Scripture presents us with a Divine Love that is all-encompassing. It is at once our Progenitor, Protector, and Provider, as well as our intimate Companion, Friend, and Lover. For this reason, we are encouraged to see ourselves as the "Beloved" of God. As Henri Nouwen reminds us, this begins with an unswerving understanding that we are the "chosen child[ren] of God, precious in God's eyes, called the Beloved from all eternity, and held safe in an everlasting embrace."[52] The Spirit within us "testifies with our spirit that we are God's children"(Rom 8:16). And as His children, we, like the "Beloved" Himself, are "heirs—heirs of God and co-heirs with Christ..."(Matt 17:5 ESV; Rom 8:17).

As heirs of the Kingdom, we are also the recipients of God's intimate and devoted love for His bride: the Church (Eph 5:22-33). Though we sin and so distance ourselves from Him, He pursues us with a tireless love and an unrelenting forgiveness. In this love, He will one day come to reclaim His bride (Rev

---

[52] Henri Nouwen, *The Life of the Beloved* (New York: The Crossroad Publishing Company, 2002), 59.

22). What glorious hope this gives us! And in this hope, like John the Baptist, we are called to be "full of joy when [we] hear the Bridegroom's voice"(John 3:29).

Until He comes, however, Scripture exhorts our efforts towards joyful obedience. We are called to find the privilege of daily demonstrating an obedient love to the One who loves us beyond measure. In short: We are invited to write a love story of obedience with our lives.

If the story we write is one of true love, it will embrace God and His will. It will hunger for nothing less! Indeed, as Merton notes, "an efficacious desire to love God makes us turn away from everything that is opposed to His will."[53] When we are then filled with this desire, joyful obedience willingly follows.

With this natural progression as our goal, let us write our love stories to *Abba*. Let us yearn to bring a smile to His face through our loving obedience. May we be inspired to see God's commands as an opportunity to demonstrate our adoration of Him rather than an onerous burden that must be carried. Where others might complain, resist, or disobey, let us joyfully claim the opportunity to evidence our devotion to Him. Like Christ before us, let us choose at every opportunity to *obey* in love. In the resulting *joy of obeying*, we might then declare with John the Baptist, "That joy is mine, and it is now complete"(John 3:29)!

---

[53]Thomas Merton, *No Man is an Island* (New York: Harcourt, 1983), 180.

9.

Joy: The Top of Heaven's Stairway

You [God] have made known to me the path of life;
You will fill me with joy in your presence,
With eternal pleasures at your right hand.
—Psalm 16:11

Then you will look and be radiant,
Your heart will throb and swell with joy.
—Isaiah 60:5

Even when love illuminates our hearts, true joy is still somehow indescribable. Perhaps that is why G.K. Chesterton says, "Joy…is the gigantic secret of the Christian."[54] Contrary to popular opinion, it is not some warm and fuzzy feeling. It is not even "happiness," for that emotion does not do it justice. It is, rather, an unbridled rejoicing, an overwhelming exuberance, an exultation of delight, and a jubilation of spirit so profound it brings with it an unearthly and stabilizing *gravitas*: divine peace. Joy is a taste of heaven itself.

So how then can something so rapturous have any association with everyday obeying? When David cries out, "I take joy in doing your will, my God…," and "Your statues…are the joy of my heart"(Ps 40:8 NLT; Ps 119:111), are these the delusional ravings of a zealot or the definitive and intentional declarations of a

---

[54] G.K. Chesterton, *Orthodoxy* (Peabody: Hendrickson Publishers, 2006), 155.

heart in love? Is the *joy of obeying* God's desire for our lives?

In answer to these questions, Scripture repeatedly reminds us of the relationship between obedience and joy. Several salient examples surface in the Old Testament when joyful obedience emerges on the heels of Israel's prior disobedience. One of these examples focuses on the character of Hezekiah. Under the reign of his father, King Ahaz, the people of Judah sinned greatly against God. Ahaz even "sacrificed his sons in the fire, following the detestable ways of the nations the Lord had driven out before the Israelites"(2 Chron 28:3).

But despite this legacy of sin, King Hezekiah survived the sacrificial fires and succeeded his father as king of Judah. As he took the throne he then committed himself and his nation to godly obedience. Hezekiah repaired the Temple of the Lord. He then purified it and consecrated its articles. Finally, he obediently initiated the sacrifices and burnt offerings pleasing to the Lord before he led Jerusalem in the Passover celebration (2 Chron 29). Calling the people to this commemoration he said, "Serve the Lord your God, so that His fierce anger will turn away from you"(2 Chron 30:8).

When the people answered Hezekiah's call to this godly obedience, "There was great joy in Jerusalem, for since the days of Solomon son of David king of Israel there had been nothing like this in Jerusalem"(2 Chron 30:26). Where children had recently been sacrificed in the fire under the reign of Ahaz, the people now found the *joy of obeying* God.

A story with similar effect can be found in the writings of Nehemiah. When the people begin to return from the Babylonian exile, Nehemiah leads them in rebuilding the walls of Jerusalem. Together with

Ezra the priest and others, they diligently and obediently set themselves to God's work. After much opposition, they ultimately complete the wall. In the midst of their faithful obedience they find this truth: "the joy of the Lord is your strength"(Neh 8:10).

The prophet Isaiah also speaks to this *joy of obeying* the Lord. After castigating the people of Israel for their insincere fasting, Isaiah goes on to describe true fasting and the importance of honoring the Sabbath. He says, "'If you keep your feet from breaking the Sabbath and from doing as you please on my holy day, if you call the Sabbath a delight and the Lord's holy day honorable, and if you honor it by not going your own way and not doing as you please or speaking idle words, then you will find your joy in the Lord…"(Is 58:13-14). Isaiah reminds us: Obedience brings God's joy into our lives.

Perhaps the greatest example of this truth resides, not surprisingly, in Jesus Christ Himself. In the middle of His parable on the vine and the branches, Jesus tells His disciples to remain in His love as the branches remain in the vine. Importantly, He further tells them the secret to remaining in Him: obeying His commands (John 15:10). Using Himself as an example Jesus says, "If you *obey* my commands, you will remain in my love, just as I have obeyed my Father's commands and remain in His love"(v. 10).

But then comes the best part—*joy*! Referring directly to His invitation to *obey*, Jesus goes on to say, "I have told you this so that my joy may be in you and that your joy may be complete"(v. 11). Jesus tells us His joy is rooted in obeying the Father and remaining in His love. *When we similarly choose to obey, Christ's joy then becomes ours, and our joy becomes complete!* We are unified with Christ as Christ is unified with the Father. In this "presence of God," we can then hope to live out our lives in "continual joy."[55] For, the indescribable—"an inexpressible and glorious joy…"(1 Pet 1:8)—takes residence within us and blossoms. What greater reason to find joy in obeying than the gift of joy itself?

In this expectation, we find the perspective to engage obedience even in the midst of life's fiercest trials. When the Apostle James says, "Consider it pure joy…whenever you face trials of many kinds, because you know that the testing of your faith develops perseverance," and "Perseverance must finish its work so that you may be mature and complete, not lacking anything," he speaks to the mysterious *joy of obeying* that emerges through affliction (Jam 1:2-3, 4). The testing that comes to our lives sharpens our obedience through perseverance. Our perseverant obedience then brings us to completion in joy.

As we consider this hard truth, let us remember again Christ's example: "Let us fix our eyes on Jesus, the Author and Perfecter of our faith, who for the joy set before Him, endured the cross, scorning its shame…"(Heb 12:2). For joy, Christ obeyed. Will we?

If we do choose to joyfully *obey* our Lord with our lives, our obedience will inspire others to *obey* just as surely as Christ's obedience inspires our own. Perhaps (and I mean no disrespect to our Lord in saying this) even more. And here is what I mean. We understand Christ is God and perfect in His obedience. But we are far from perfect, and Christ's example can sometimes seem daunting. So when we, therefore, in our imperfection, choose to *obey*, there is a human "realness" and accessibility to our everyday obedience that may become inspirational to others. Christ's example becomes alive in our imperfection. And that is exactly what God intends for our lives.

---

[55] Brother Lawrence, *The Practice of the Presence of God* (Public Domain).

Paul alludes to this wonderful mystery in his letter to the Church at Philippi. Although he longs to depart and be with Christ, he obediently understands the necessity of remaining in the body for their encouragement (Phil 1:23-24). He says, "I will continue with all of you for your progress and joy in the faith, so that through my being with you again your joy in Christ Jesus will overflow on account of me"(v. 25-26). As Paul suggests, joy can beget joy. It has an infectious quality to it. This even holds true when it comes to the topic of obedience.

But this joy will still ultimately elude us as long as our wills contend against God's will in our lives. Joy will not likely emerge from the sparks of discontent and selfishness. As Thomas Merton reminds us, "Sanctity...consists in willing the will of God."[56] Christ did this perfectly. He came down from heaven to do God's will, the very food of His soul (John 6:39, 4:34).

When our hearts, like Christ's, truly will God's will, obedience becomes privilege and pleasure! It is no longer an onerous compulsion, but a natural overflow of the Spirit's exuberance within us. Love abounds. Joy is born. And our lives become, in a sense, like Beethoven's 9th Symphony: a triumphal "Ode to Joy."

Composed in the midst of complete deafness, Beethoven's imaginative "inner ear" obeyed the Spirit's inspiration and His musical, mathematical laws to create a symphony that sings joyful praise to God. Beethoven might have been physically weak—"handicapped" for his work. But in that weakness, God's joyful strength blossomed as Beethoven's spirit willed God's will within him to create a masterpiece, one silent note at a time. And in this process, our Lord's words rang true in his

---

[56]Thomas Merton, *No Man is an Island* (New York: Harcourt, 1983), 56.

life: "My grace is sufficient for you, for my power is made perfect in weakness"(2 Cor 12:9-11). The Lord undoubtedly delighted to empower Beethoven's crowning efforts!

In a similar way, every decision for obedience in our lives carries with it the hope of bringing a smile to our *Abba*. We are composing life symphonies. And while we might, like Beethoven, have imperfect bodies or broken hearts, our imperfection can also be empowered to *obey*. One note after the next, one feeble step in front of the other, we have the opportunity to build towards a joyful, choral crescendo for a Father whose radiant love draws us close. And in that proximity, "It is the joy of ever hearing the Father's voice that will give the joy and strength of true obedience."[57]

Strengthened in this manner, we can then delight in the *joy of obeying,* knowing that He is well pleased with our willing submission: "for God loves a cheerful giver"(2 Cor 9:7). We can go about our daily business joyfully obeying "purely for the love of God," and no other reason.[58]

When our loving obedience falls short of this mark, God has provided ample helpers to enthuse our devotion. The encouragements of blessing, fear, pain, shame, duty, respect, and even the examples of creation itself, can help empower our flagging efforts to *obey*. These forces may assist our obedience until we are capable of freely and joyfully willing God's will in our lives with the power of Christ's perfect love.

As we are lifted towards this higher love of obeying our Father, we begin to understand why C.S.

---

[57] Andrew Murray, *The School of Obedience* (Public Domain).

[58] Brother Lawrence, *The Practice of the Presence of God* (Public Domain).

Lewis says, "obedience is the stairway of pleasure...."[59] At the top, robed in the perfection Christ has purchased for us, we shall stand complete in His joy. Have we not been assured, "The prospect of the righteous is joy..."(Prov 10:28)? And is God not "able to keep you from falling and to present you before His glorious presence without fault and with great joy..."(Jude 1:24)?

Bathed in Christ's radiant glory, we will then know without a doubt, "Joy is the serious business of heaven."[60] We will come to the final realization of what we might have known all along: We were created to write a love story to God with our lives, penned in the *joy of obeying.*

---

[59] C.S. Lewis, *That Hideous Strength* (New York: Scribner Paperback Fiction, 1996), 63.

[60] C.S. Lewis, *Letters to Malcom* in *The Business of Heaven* (New York: HarperCollins, 1984), 5.

Collected Readings

Introduction

Andrew Murray, *The School of Obedience* (Public Domain).

C.S. Lewis, *Mere Christianity* (New York: HarperCollins, 1980).

C.S. Lewis, *Perelandra* in *The Space Trilogy* (London: HarperCollins, 2013).

Francis Chan, *Letters to the Church* (Colorado Springs: David C Cook, 2018).

Francois Mauriac, *The Desert of Love* in *A Mauriac Reader* (New York: Farrar, Straus and Giroux, 1968).

Soren Kierkegaard, *The Lily of the Field and the Bird of the Air* (Princeton: Princeton University Press, 2016).

Chapter 1

Andrew Murray, *The School of Obedience* (Public Domain).

Graham Greene, *The Heart of the Matter* (New York: Penguin Books, 1999).

Soren Kierkegaard, *Fear and Trembling* (London: Penguin Books, 2003).

Chapter 2

Ken Stead, "Fear Has No Place Here," *Fear Has No Place Here,* 2015.

Chapter 3

Andrew Murray, *Absolute Surrender* (Public Domain).

Andrew Murray, *The School of Obedience* (Public Domain).

C.S. Lewis, *Perelandra* in *The Space Trilogy* (London: HarperCollins, 2013).

Oswald Chambers, *My Utmost for His Highest* (Grand Rapids: Discovery House, 1992).

Soren Kierkegaard, *The Lily of the Field and the Bird of the Air* (Princeton: Princeton University Press, 2016).

Chapter 4

Andrew Murray, *The School of Obedience* (Public Domain).

C.S. Lewis, *The Problem of Pain* (New York: HarperCollins, 1996).

Soren Kierkegaard, *Fear and Trembling* (London: Penguin Books, 2003).

Thomas Merton, *No Man is an Island* (New York: Harcourt, 1983).

Chapter 5

Andrew Murray, *Absolute Surrender* (Public Domain).

Andrew Murray, *The School of Obedience* (Public Domain).

C.S. Lewis, *The Problem of Pain* (New York: HarperCollins, 1996).

Dante Alighieri, *Inferno* (Public Domain).

Dietrich Bonhoeffer, *Ethics* (New York: Simon & Schuster, 1995).

Chapter 6

A.W. Tozer, *The Pursuit of God* in *The Classic Works of A.W. Tozer* (Public Domain).

Chapter 7

Oswald Chambers, *Baffled to Fight Better* in *The Complete Works of Oswald Chambers* (Grand Rapids: Discovery House, 2000).

Soren Kierkegaard, *The Lily of the Field and the Bird of the Air* (Princeton: Princeton University Press, 2016).

Thomas Merton, *No Man is an Island* (New York: Harcourt, 1983).

Chapter 8

C.S. Lewis, 'The Grand Miracle,' *God in the Dock* in *The Business of Heaven* (New York: HarperCollins, 1984).

Henri Nouwen, *The Life of the Beloved* (New York: The Crossroad Publishing Company, 2002).

Rainer Rilke, *Rilke's Book of Hours: Love Poems to God* (New York: Riverhead Books, 2005).

Soren Kierkegaard, *The Lily of the Field and the Bird of the Air* (Princeton: Princeton University Press, 2016).

Thomas Merton, *No Man is an Island* (New York: Harcourt, 1983).

Chapter 9

Andrew Murray, *The School of Obedience* (Public Domain).

Brother Lawrence, *The Practice of the Presence of God* (Public Domain).

C.S. Lewis, *That Hideous Strength* (New York: Scribner Paperback Fiction, 1996).

C.S. Lewis, *Letters to Malcom* in *The Business of Heaven* (New York: HarperCollins, 1984).

G.K. Chesterton, *Orthodoxy* (Peabody: Hendrickson Publishers, 2006).

Thomas Merton, *No Man is an Island* (New York: Harcourt, 1983).

Acknowledgements

I am so very grateful to my Editors, Gail K. Eubanks, PhD., and William A. Eubanks, MA. Your support of this project and God's work in my life are a constant gift to me. Love you.

I am thankful for the family and friends—Mike, Liz, Jeff, Helga, Kevin and others—who have given their time, prayer, and support to my life and God's work in and through me.

I am grateful for Elise and Adele. Your inquisitive minds and tender hearts helped inspire this love story.

I am eternally indebted to the Father who calls me "Beloved," the Savior who calls me "Brother" and "Friend," and the Spirit who calls my heart "Home." I love you Lord.

ABOUT THE AUTHOR

Dr. Eubanks is blessed to be a child of God who delights in obeying his heavenly Father. His mission field is currently medicine, where he is an Associate Professor of Orthopaedic Surgery at Case Western Reserve University School of Medicine and the Chief of Spine Surgery at University Hospitals Ahuja Medical Center. He is the author of *More of Him, Less of Me: A Doctor's Devotional for Spiritual Health* and a volume of poetry entitled, *Rotations: A Medical Student's Clinical Experience.* He has written over 20 peer-reviewed scientific publications, multiple textbook chapters and editorials, and poetry appearing in journals such as *JAMA*, *The Annals of Internal Medicine*, *Tar River Poetry*, and more. He lives outside of Cleveland, Ohio.

www.ingramcontent.com/pod-product-compliance
Lightning Source LLC
Chambersburg PA
CBHW031453040426
42444CB00007B/1082